THE CHICAGO PUBLIC LIBRARY

FORM 19

HEALERS

by
Irene M. Franck
and
David M. Brownstone

A Volume in the Work Throughout History Series

Facts On File
New York • Oxford

Healers

Copyright © 1989 by Irene M. Franck and David M. Brownstone

Facts On File
460 Park Avenue South
New York, NY 10016

Library of Congress Cataloging-in-Publication Data

Franck, Irene M.
  Healers / by Irene M. Franck and David M. Brownstone.
    p.   cm. — (Work throughout history)
  Bibliography: p.
  Includes index.
  Summary: Explores the role throughout history of the occupations involved with healing, including barbers, midwives, psychologists, and veterinarians.
  ISBN 0-8160-1446-9
  1.   Medical personnel—History—Juvenile literature. 2. Healers—History—Juvenile literature. [1. Medical personnel—History. 2. Healers—History. 3. Occupations—History.]   I. Brownstone, David M.   II. Title.   III. Series
  R690.F713   1989
  610.69—dc19   88-26776

British CIP data available on request
Jacket Design by Richard Oriolo
Composition by Facts On File, Inc.
Printed in the United States of America

10 9 8 7 6 5 4 3 2 1

Contents

Preface

Healers is a book in the multivolume series, *Work Throughout History*. Work shapes the lives of all human beings; yet surprisingly little has been written about the history of the many fascinating and diverse types of occupations men and women pursue. The books in the *Work Throughout History* series explore humanity's most interesting, important, and influential occupations. They explain how and why these occupations came into being in the major cultures of the world, how they evolved over the centuries, especially with changing technology, and how society's view of each occupation has changed. Throughout we focus on what it was like to do a particular kind of work—for example, to be a farmer, glassblower, midwife, banker, building contractor, actor, astrologer, or weaver—in centuries past and right up to today.

Because many occupations have been closely related to one another, we have included at the end of each article references to other, overlapping occupations. In preparing this series, we have drawn on a wide range of general works on social, economic, and occupational history, including many on everyday life throughout history. We consulted far too many wide-ranging works to list them all here; but at the end of each volume is a list of suggestions for further reading, should readers want to learn more about any of the occupations included in the volume.

Many researchers and writers worked on the preparation of this series. For *Healers*, David G. Merrill was the primary researcher-writer for parts of this volume. Our thanks go to him for his fine work; to our expert typists, Shirley Fenn, Nancy Fishelberg, and Mary Racette; to our most helpful editors at Facts On File, first Kate Kelly and then James Warren, and their assistant Claire Johnston and later Barbara Levine; to our excellent developmental editor, Vicki Tyler; and to our publisher, Edward Knappman, who first suggested the *Work Throughout History* series and has given us gracious support during the long years of its preparation.

We also express our special appreciation to the many librarians whose help has been indispensable in completing this work, especially to the incomparable staff of the Chappaqua Library—director Mark Hasskarl and former director Doris Lowenfels; the reference staff, including Mary Platt, Paula Peyraud, Terry Cullen, Martha Alcott, Carolyn Jones, and formerly Helen Barolini, Karen Baker, and Linda Goldstein; Jane McKean, Caroline Chojnowski, Marcia Van Fleet, and the whole circulation staff—and the many other librarians who, throughout the Interlibrary Loan network, have provided us with the research tools so vital to our work.

Irene M. Franck
David M. Brownstone

Introduction

The healers form one of the oldest families of human occupations, dating back at least to the apparent "medicine man" shown on the wall of a cave in Europe over 15,000 years ago, and probably much earlier than that, to the first time a bone was set or a hot pack applied. *Physicians and surgeons* were closely associated with religion for thousands of years. Over the centuries, they performed a wide range of functions, including mixing medicines, fixing teeth, treating mental illnesses, and even caring for valuable animals. In doing this, they used various means of treatment: religious, magical, and—only gradually—scientific. They did not generally deliver children, however. The *midwife,* an occupation established long before Biblical times, usually attended mothers in labor, calling in physicians and surgeons only when necessary. Also from early times, *pharmacists* specialized in producing and selling drugs and medicines, though physicians often prepared their own.

By the time of the early Egyptian and Mesopotamian civilizations, other healing specialties had begun to develop. Physicians continued to perform most healing functions, however, as they have even into modern times. *Barbers,* skilled in the use of the knife, took over much minor surgery, in addition to their grooming activities. At certain times in history, notably during the Middle Ages in Europe, they performed almost all surgery, although often under the direction of a physician. In early India and in the Greek and Roman worlds, nursing also became a separate function. By a quirk of history, medicine and nursing were separated in the early Christian period. After that the profession of *nurse* developed independently until modern times. Then nurses were brought into a medical hierarchy with physicians and surgeons at the top.

During the Renaissance surgery was reunited with the rest of medicine. But as medicine became more complex, medical practitioners tended to specialize in a particular type of problem or patient. Some specialties—notably those of *dentist* and, more recently, *veterinarian*—split off completely. More often, specialization was a matter of advanced training in a given area, beyond basic medical training. For example, the *obstetrician* in recent centuries has largely replaced the midwife in most technologically advanced societies. And as medicine moved away from religion and focused on the treatment of physical ills by scientific means, the *psychologist* and *psychiatrist* emerged as specialists treating mental illnesses.

Barbers and Hairdressers

In the modern period, barbers and hairdressers have been mainly concerned with cutting and styling hair, shaving or trimming beards and mustaches, dressing wigs, advising on skin care and make-up, and manicuring nails. However, for many centuries, barbers perform a wide variety of other, far more varied functions, including surgery, dentistry, embalming, and tattooing.

Some of the earliest known barbers were in ancient Egypt, where men and women generally shaved their heads and wore wigs. Priests and high officials shaved off all body hair, a practice later adopted by many Greeks. Most of Egypt's royalty and wealthy citizens were cleaned, shaved, and styled by personal slaves, some of whom became specialists in dressing hair, wigs, and the body. Independent barbers tended the needs of

1

other Egyptian men, either in a shop or at the side of a street, where a customer would squat or kneel while a barber shaved him. Barbers also performed other functions requiring skill with a knife and other sharp instruments. They treated and extracted teeth, performed surgical procedures, doing minor surgery on their own and major surgery under a physician's direction, and branded slaves.

In early Greece men often wore long hair and artificially curled beards, but after the Persian Wars shorter hair became the fashion. In the time of Alexander the Great, around 330 B.C., they began to cut or shave their beards; Alexander reputedly feared that beards would serve as handles for the enemy in battle. These changes in fashion produced a skilled class of barbers, who worked in or near the market square of the Greek city-states. As Greek colonies spread around the Mediterranean Sea, so did the skilled Greek barbers, the first of them arriving in Rome from Sicily in 454 B.C. Later, as Rome gained power in the Mediterranean, many Greek barbers were imported to set up shops along the main streets of the Roman cities. Like most Greeks in early Rome, these barbers started as slaves, but some of them became so successful that they had slaves of their own as assistants and a few even owned private villas. Less prosperous barbers worked on poorer customers out in the open, in the main gathering places of the cities and towns.

Women's grooming needs were almost always tended to in the home. Those few men rich enough to keep a private stock of razors, combs, mirrors, lotions, and perfumes were shaved by personal barbers in their homes. For the rest it became the practice in Rome, as it had been in Greece, to pay a morning visit to the barbershop, where a man could hear the news of the day while being shaved, trimmed, and manicured. The barber's reputation for being talkative goes back at least to the days of Rome. One Roman citizen, when asked by the barber how he wished to be shaved, supposedly replied, "Without speaking." In fact, the process was long

This Chinese street barber is cleaning his customer's ears, as just one of his many services, using heated water from the stand to the right. (Courtesy of the Wellcome Trustees, London)

and tedious, for the tools were crude, so crude that individuals could not shave themselves. Barbers were required to undergo a long apprenticeship and they needed considerable skill to avoid gashing and gouging their clients. A strict order of merit prevailed: the worst, roughest barbers traveled the countryside; the best stayed in Rome and could name their price—and did.

Later, when many well-to-do Roman men became dandies, the simple shave was just one part of an elaborate routine that included dyeing and curling the hair, perfuming and creaming the face, and covering up blemishes. The barber, or *tonsor,* became such an important part of Roman life that a boy's first shave at the barber's was made part of a religious ceremony, the *depositio barbae,* and the shaven hairs were offered to the gods. Even the slaves in the great households were sent by their masters to be shaved by the street barbers. For several centuries, to be unshaven was to be classified as hopelessly poor, rural, even barbarian. Only during the reign of Emperor Hadrian, in the early second century A.D., did the fashion for shaving begin to become less popular.

Barbershops have been a part of settled communities all around the world. When Cortés entered Tenochtitlán, capital of Montezuma's Aztec Empire, in 1519, he reported, "You see barber shops where you can bathe and have your hair cut. . . ." Barbershops have always been public and social places, even when barbers were shaving the whole body or performing surgical operations. There have also always been traveling barbers, from early Egypt into the 20th century. Some wandered the city streets, often (as in China) ringing a bell to announce their presence; others traveled from place to place, plying their trade wherever people gathered, such as at fairs and marketplaces.

Where metal tools were scarce, the barber who owned sharp tools and was skilled in their use was called on to perform a wide variety of tasks. In some areas barbers produced ritual or ornamental scars or body tattoos. In the Mayan civilization, for example, tattooing involved painting the body and then cutting tiny gashes in the painted area to let paint and blood mingle; elsewhere needles were employed for tattooing. In societies where eunuchs were favored, barbers were employed to castrate them; such knife wielders often formed a group of social outcasts and sometimes, as in China, had to live outside the city walls. Some also specialized in gelding animals, such as hogs. Gelders were often called in by midwives to dismember an unborn dead child with their knives and remove the parts piecemeal from the mother's womb, using hooks the midwife carried for that purpose. Barbers also performed circumcisions in some parts of the world where they were not performed by priest-physicians. In addition to their standard grooming activities, they carried out such functions as cleaning ears; in China, for example, barbers first shaved hairs from the ear canal with a slender knife and then used forceps and long, sharp needles to remove remaining particles—a process that often produced punctured eardrums and infection.

Even when trained surgeons were available, poor people could rarely afford their services, so barbers filled the gap by performing emergency and minor surgery, letting blood, setting bones, and pulling teeth. Such a range of functions became the norm for European barbers after the fall of the Roman Empire, when the practice of shaving declined sharply, along with other hygienic and fashionable customs. The number of barbers declined as well, and those who remained focused more and more on their nongrooming activities.

Many barbers were attached to the medieval hospitals that developed near monasteries. These hospitals were places of refuge not only for the sick, as they are today, but also for the poor, the homeless, the aged, the orphaned, and the traveler. These barbers performed many caretaking functions now carried out by nurses or orderlies, especially in the men's wards of convent hospitals. They also shaved the monks' faces and tonsures, which were the round areas at the top of the head. (While most European men went bearded, members of the medieval Christian clergy were clean-shaven, according to church policy, which lasted into the 16th century.) Many barbers also worked at public baths, which were often near the hospitals. People came to these baths, especially thermal baths, for a variety of treatments.

In this period operations were regarded as manual work beneath the dignity of a physician. So physicians, most of whom were monks in this period, often called upon barbers to perform operations. While physicians prescribed operations and identified which cuts should be made where, the actual cutting was done by barbers—even though these barbers were often illiterate and had no medical training, only practical experience learned in apprenticeship.

But the keystone of the barber's trade in medieval

times was bloodletting. Bleeding was performed for a wide variety of reasons, such as when there was thought to be an excess of one of the "four humors" (blood, phlegm, black bile, and yellow bile), which were believed to control the body. Lovesickness and melancholy were often considered reasons for bleeding, and it was said that in some courts ladies were bled to keep them from blushing at bawdy stories. Barbers were responsible for the periodic bleeding of monks, for which they were given a special title: *rasor et minutor* (barber and remover of blood). Many people went to their local barber for bleeding, without benefit of physician, every spring and fall, as someone today might have an automobile tuned up. The traditional symbol of the barber's trade, the red-and-white striped pole, was originally an advertisement of the barber's bloodletting activities: a bloody bandage wrapped around the pole used to steady a patient's arm.

Bloodletting was done in a variety of ways. One widespread method of removing blood involved placing a cup over an open cut in the body. Thought to be most beneficial after bathing, cupping was so common that bleeders who worked in baths were often called *cuppers* or *bathers*. Leeches were also used to suck blood from patients, and up to the 19th century, anyone who performed bleeding operations might also be called a *leech*. (In early history the term was not necessarily negative; Homer, for example, called Greek surgeons "noble leeches.") Most often, however, barbers simply cut a patient's vein to let blood. Physicians used astrology to indicate where to bleed a patient, depending on the date and the patient's zodiacal sign. But since many barbers were unable to read, astrological charts were prepared for them to follow.

After a papal decree in 1163 forbade members of the clergy from drawing blood with a knife, surgery passed almost entirely into the hands of untrained, mostly illiterate barber-surgeons. In addition to doing almost all surgical and dental operations, barbers also performed embalmings and autopsies, both of which were rare until modern times, and continued working in even more unsavory capacities, as executioners, gelders, and torturers. In this period the barber's reputation fell to a very low level, so low that in medieval Germany a prospective apprentice had to swear that he came from honest, married parents and a family that included no barbers, bathers, or skinners. The public felt more kindly toward barbers in the 14th century, when many physicians fled from the plague epidemic called the Black Death, while most barbers stayed behind. These

This 14th-century "short-robed" barber-surgeon is bleeding a patient. A bloody rag wrapped around the pole used to steady the patient's arm became the barber's symbol, the striped pole. (British Library, London, Add. Ms. 42130, fol. 61)

barber-surgeons were not necessarily more noble, and possibly only less mobile, but they did what they could. Unfortunately, by lancing the boils of the plague victims, they probably unknowingly helped spread the disease.

Gradually barbers came to be in more demand for their shaving and haircutting skills. Following the example of the clergy, shaving was adopted by more and more laymen. The practice spread widely with successive migrations; the Normans, for example, reintroduced the fashion of shaving into England. Some barbers became trusted confidants and powerful men in their own right, as did many people who performed personal services for the ruling classes. People had a lingering fear of the power of the knife, however. Certainly legends of mad barbers, like Sweeney Todd, who killed their clients with a razor, have been widespread in northern Europe for hundreds of years.

As secular universities began to emerge in Europe in the 12th and 13th centuries, and as anatomy and surgery gradually became part of a course of medical study, the by now enlarged group of barbers began to split into two groups: the academically trained *surgeons* and the *barber-surgeons*. The distinction between them was formalized first in France during the early 13th century, when the educated surgeons became "the surgeons of the long robe," which was the robe given to people with university degrees, and the barber-surgeons became "the surgeons of the short robe," which was the short jerkin worn by the ordinary people in Europe at that time. The description was apt, for, despite their sometimes bloody occupations, these practitioners wore no protective covering, only clothing reflecting their social status.

The academic surgeons and the barber-surgeons coexisted uneasily for the next few centuries. Like other tradespeople, they began to form guilds, controlling those who practiced the same skills. In some places the barbers and surgeons formed united guilds, as they did in France in 1361; elsewhere they formed separate guilds. In England—where the Master of the first local Barber's Company in 1308 was, appropriately enough, Richard le Barbour—the barbers formed a general guild in 1462 and then merged with the surgeon's guild in 1540, during the reign of Henry VIII. Because barbers were in competition with surgeons, guild wardens were especially strict in inspecting the work and instruments of the barbers in a guild's area. In addition, the guilds worked to protect barber-surgeons from others who might try to take on their rights and privileges; for example, in the 17th century, when embalming began to be more common, the charter for one English barber-surgeon guild specified that only their members could perform this job. Barbers also became pawns in the battle between physicians and surgeons. (See separate article on Physicians and Surgeons.) In some areas, physicians wanted to keep surgeons in a subordinate position, and, when surgeons resisted, physicians used barbers as assistants instead. Although barbers were generally excluded from universities, some schools provided special lectures for those who were to assist physicians. Such assistants were intended to relieve physicians from having to answer urgent calls personally, which the physicians considered a slavish chore.

During this period barbering was not an exclusively male occupation. Women barbers, although always outnumbered by their male counterparts, practiced throughout Europe. Many were wives or daughters of male barbers who learned and practiced their trade in the family. That such a practice was common is indicated by a directive of the Archbishop of Canterbury in 1413 that no barber, his wife, son, daughter, apprentice, or servant should work at haircutting or shaving on Sundays. Some women, after apprenticeship, set up their own shops. The Paris tax rolls of 1292, for example, list 12 *barbieres* (female barbers); five women barbers in Drury Lane were celebrated in a popular London song; and the records of the barbers' guild for Lincoln, England refer to the "brothers and sisters of the guild." The patron

While the barber trims the locks of one customer, his assistant washes the hair of another, in this 16th-century shop surrounded by barbering implements. (By Jost Amman, from The Book of Trades, *late 16th century)*

saints of barbers were two early Christian martyrs, St. Cosmas and St. Damian.

Certain barber-surgeons came to be highly skilled at performing surgical operations. The Frenchman Ambroise Paré, who is considered the father of modern surgery, began as a traveling barber-surgeon in the 16th century. In 1505 barber-surgeons were admitted to the faculty of the University of Paris. Gradually, however, barbers and surgeons diverged sharply, and those barbers who cut or shaved hair were not allowed to perform surgery. This practice was made law in France in 1743 and in England in 1745. In England the Royal College of Surgeons was founded in 1800, although the last practicing barber-surgeon in England did not die until 1821. Dentistry, too, was gradually taken out of the

These wigmakers (in French, perruquiers) are making and tending wigs for their fashionable clients shortly before the French Revolution. (From Diderot's Encyclopedia, late 18th century)

barber's hands, becoming the separate occupation of surgeon-dentist in the 17th century.

In developed countries, the barber's activities thereafter were mostly confined to care of the hair, scalp, and nails. The barber's trade did not diminish, however, because the public was becoming more and more conscious of grooming. The barber's shop once more became a social gathering place—many barbers even kept guitars in their shops so customers could while away the waiting time playing so-called "barber's music." Fashionable men would gather in the barbershops to have their hair trimmed in the latest style—and their beards and mustaches as well, as these passed in and out of style over the years. In this period, barbers who specialized in shaving and haircutting began to wear aprons with pockets for their various implements; in some parts of Europe checkered aprons were so common that by the end of the 16th century a barber was sometimes called the "checkered apron man."

Barbers were never backward about advertising their functions. In earlier times many used to put bowls of blood in their shop windows to alert potential patients to their bloodletting capabilities. Londoners found that practice so offensive that in 1307 they passed a law instructing barbers to have the blood "privately carried into the Thames under the pain of paying two shillings to the use of the Sheriffs." Even so, as late as 1727, John Gay gave the following description of a barber's shop in his fable, "The Goat Without a Beard":

His pole, with pewter basins hung,
Black, rotten teeth in order strung,
Rang'd cups that in the window stood,
Lin'd with red rags, to look like blood,
Did well his threefold trade explain,
Who shav'd, drew teeth, and breath'd a vein.

The fashion for wigs in the 17th and 18th centuries created a whole new range of activities for barbers: they now became *wigmakers* and *wig stylers*. Wigmakers even formed a separate guild in France. Wigs were usually fashioned from real hair, bought from poor people who sold their hair or sometimes taken from the dead. Samuel Pepys in 1665 thought that the mania for wigs would pass because people would fear that hair used to make them might have been taken from plague victims. But the fashion survived, and to it was added an extra element: powdering, which caused many barbers to adopt a white apron. These wigs were such valuable property that thieves developed a method of stealing them on the street: a small child riding on a man's shoulders would snatch the wigs from the heads of passers-by. The wig craze also crossed the ocean, with barbers exporting wigs to wealthy landowners in the Americas. Demand was such that some European wigmakers moved to the colonies. By 1769 eight British wigmakers had settled in Williamsburg, Virginia.

While many men brought their wigs to the barbershops

for dressing, the fashion for wigs provided barbers with a new clientele: women. Barbers were often called to the homes of the fashionable and wealthy to dress the men's wigs and to style the elaborate hairstyles or *coiffures* of the women. Some of the women's hair arrangements rose as high as three feet into the air, on elaborate constructions of cages, springs, and pads. They took several hours to prepare and sometimes stayed in place for one to three weeks. Since such a long-term hair arrangement, covered with flour and treated with various oils, tended to attract vermin, the wearers often put a dab of honey and vinegar in the top of the hairdo—to attract lice and fleas away from their scalps.

Creating such elaborate constructions was obviously a specialty and the barbers who styled them gradually came to be known as *hairdressers* or *hair stylists*. These hairdressers were much in demand and were often catapulted from rags to riches. A French hairdresser named Champagne, for example, was "discovered" by a countess while he was rearranging the hair of a shepherdess injured in a fall. Champagne even opened a ladies' hairdressing salon in Paris. Although it was censured by church figures, the salon was a great success with the royal and the rich, closing only upon his death. Champagne was the first of a long line of celebrity hairdressers, who today cater to the jet set and movie stars. In the same period, some women, including Madame Martin of Paris, also became fashionable hairdressers.

Thereafter, the term "barber" was applied primarily to males who tended male customers, while women barbers and barbers of either sex who handled women's hair were often called *hairdressers* or *hair stylists*. Hairdressing specialists even began to write books and open schools. For example, Legros de Rumigny, a former baker who became wigmaker and hairdresser to the French court, wrote a widely circulated fashion guide and in 1769 founded the Academie de Coiffure, where he taught men and women hairdressers over three dozen of his original hairdressing designs, employing beautiful young women to show off his creations in public. He also gave less complete classes—for smaller fees—to *valets* and *chambermaids*, who served as hairdressers to their employers at home.

Barbers and hairdressers alike were subject to a number of special laws regarding powdered wigs. In an attempt to control hairdressing compounds, the British Parliament passed a law specifying that wig powder should be made of starch and include no plaster of paris, lime, or other such materials. It imposed a tax on the powder per pound, which was doubled for powder made of imported starch. Wigs, in fact, grew so popular that some governments, desperate for new means to raise money, taxed hair powder, as William Pitt the Younger did in 1795. Partly as a reaction to these taxes and to the shortage of flour after some poor harvests, as well as the association of wigs with the aristocracy in the period following the French Revolution, wigs passed out of fashion. Wigmakers thrown out of work staged demonstrations in some places, but contemporary observers noted that their cause was hurt by the demonstrators themselves being wigless. Some people continued to wear powdered wigs, among them butlers, who were obliged to wear wigs for another century. In some places wigs remained a sign of office, as is still true among judges, barristers, and bishops in England today.

In modern times, the barber's activities have been more restricted. As men's hairstyles became simpler, customers had less need for elaborate skills, and barbering was commonly along the lines of "a shave and a haircut—two bits." Male patrons still frequented barbershops—indeed the regulars had their own personal shaving mugs lined up in the barber's window. But that practice, too, declined when an American named King C. Gillette invented the safety razor, introduced in 1903. These razors were cheap and disposable and allowed men to shave themselves easily and safely at home. The barbershop was still a social center, however. Men came not only for haircuts and the occasional shave but also for the latest news and sometimes for entertainment. The barbershop quartet, which was especially popular in turn-of-the-century America, is thought to have developed from the practice of patrons harmonizing popular songs while waiting for their turn in the barber's chair. Indeed, some popular singers—such as Perry Como, the "singing barber"—got their start behind the barber's chair.

Hairdressers, however, still had a wide circle of patrons. Although wigs were out, fashion generally dictated somewhat elaborate styles for women's natural hair. Until World War I, hairdressers continued to visit their affluent women customers in their homes. For such visits they dressed in formal clothes, without aprons, although in barbershops they usually worked in shirt sleeves, with aprons and sleeve protectors. New techniques did entice some women into the few hairdressing salons, however. French hairdresser Marcel Grateau introduced the Marcel wave, formed by a curling iron, in the 1870s. After providing free hairstyling to show off the new wave, he drew the patronage of some famous and fashionable people, and his Parisian salon became a huge success. The permanent wave process, developed by Charles Nestle (born Karl Nessler, son of a German shoemaker) in 1905, provided many new possibilities for hairstyling.

In the 1920s, as social restrictions on women decreased, hairdressing shops for women became widespread. Many barbers and hairdressers adopted white uniforms similar to those of medical practitioners, although the most fashionable of them continued to wear formal clothes. Women were sometimes employed as *manicurists* and as barber's assistants, to lather up customers before the barber did the actual shaving. Around this time, barbering began to come under government restrictions.

In the United States, barbers—those who simply give shaves and haircuts—must be licensed graduates of barber's schools. Hairdressers—those who dye hair or give permanents or other cosmetic treatments—must be licensed graduates of cosmetology schools. In many parts of Europe, barbers and hairdressers are required to serve as apprentices for one to five years before being allowed to register for independent practice. Although wandering street barbers continue to operate in many parts of the world, barbershops and hairdressing shops are becoming the norm, as part of a broad process of Westernization.

While barbers and hairdressers are distinguished in the popular mind, they are generally members of the same trade organizations, and the distinctions between them have blurred somewhat in the last several decades. As men's hairstyles have become longer and more elaborate, some barbers have attended cosmetology schools in order to qualify to dye, wave, and set men's hair—not just shave and cut it. Conversely, women who want short, simple haircuts have sometimes turned to barbers. The 20th century has also seen a revival of wigs—not elaborate powdered affairs but naturally styled wigs for women and toupees and hairpieces for both sexes. Although 20th-century wigmaking is centered mainly in Hong Kong—where labor is cheap and hair plentiful, sold by poor people—modern barbers and hairdressers fit, style, and dress the wigs.

Some other specialties have developed from the practice of barbering. Modern specialists in the treatment of hair and scalp call themselves *trichologists,* or *hair-and-scalp treatment specialists*. In addition to treating scalp conditions, they also use such new techniques as hair weaving and implantation. Now more respectable than the old street barkers selling potions and lotions for surefire hair growth, these specialists now are subject to government regulations. They were able to establish a specialty primarily because medical practitioners—in their desire to separate themselves from barbers—paid relatively little attention to hair and scalp problems until this century.

This 1920's hairdresser sports the latest gadget in his field—a permanent wave machine. (Library of Congress)

Tattoo artists have also split off as a distinct specialty. Tattooing has been practiced all over the world, from as early as 2000 B.C. in Egypt. It has often been used for tribal identification or ritual ornamentation and as a method of marking criminals, prostitutes, and slaves at various times in history. In recent centuries, tattooing has enjoyed some minor fashion vogue in the Western world.

A specialty resulting from the development of the

modern electric needles is electrolysis. The *electrolysist* uses electrified needles to kill and permanently remove unwanted hair. Although they sometimes set up their own shops, electrolysists often work in hairdressing salons. In the developed countries today, hairdressers (sometimes called *beauticians* or *cosmetologists*) generally outnumber barbers. In the United States the ratio is approximately four to one; in the late 1970s there were over 500,000 cosmetologists to nearly 125,000 barbers. About one-third to one-half of these specialists own their own businesses, while the rest work in shops owned by others or are employed by governments, hotels, department stores, or hospitals. Some barbers and beauticians also assist *undertakers* in preparing bodies for burial. Since many cosmetic and hairdressing techniques today apply to both sexes, some barbers and hairdressers have opened unisex salons, catering to both men and women customers. As always, they remain subject to the whims and dictates of fashion.

For related occupations in this volume, *Healers,* see the following:
Dentists
Midwives and Obstetricians
Nurses
Pharmacists
Physicians and Surgeons

For related occupations in other volumes of the series, see the following:
in *Helpers and Aides:*
Bath Workers
Undertakers

Dentists

People who practiced dentistry were at one time known as "toothers," a not inappropriate name. Three thousand years before the birth of Christ, the earliest dental practitioner on record, Hesi-Re of Saqqara in Egypt, was officially known as "Chief of the Toothers and Physicians." Hesi-Re and his colleagues were not solely dentists. Dentistry is a relatively recent medical specialty. As a separate occupation, it is less than 300 years old. For most of human history, dental problems were treated by *physicians* and *barber-surgeons*.

Clay tables from Sumer, in what is now Iraq, are the first to describe toothaches, in about 2500 B.C. The Sumerians believed that dental decay was caused by worms, a belief that persists in some parts of the world even today. In this early period, dental problems were treated primarily with incantations by priest-physicians who hoped to exorcise the pain-causing demons, but medicines and some crude surgical techniques were used as well. Because dental treatment, like other surgery, was considered manual work, it was usually performed not by physicians but by barber-surgeons. These barber-surgeons were jacks of many trades, with dental work only one of their functions.

The civilizations of early India had practitioners who excelled in surgery, including dental work. Their training included practical experience in pulling teeth from the jaws of dead animals. Hindu specialists, alert to the need for prevention of dental problems, recommended that their patients clean their teeth with wood from certain trees now known to have medicinal properties. Indian barber-surgeons drilled holes in decayed teeth and, working with *jewelers,* then filled the cavities with gold or jewels—only for the richest patients, of course. In China, as early as 2700 B.C., some dental problems were treated with acupuncture (piercing the body with needles), as they still are in parts of East Asia. In the Near East, dental specialists also replaced teeth that had been lost or extracted. The early Jews fashioned teeth out of gold, silver, or wood; the Greeks and Romans made artificial teeth of ivory; and some other people, such as the Phoenicians, replaced the lost teeth of the rich with healthy teeth extracted from the mouths of slaves. Physicians carried out some of these dental procedures, particularly on royalty or very wealthy patients, but most dental operations—which were primarily extractions, scraping plaque off teeth, and treating jaw wounds—continued to be carried out by barber-surgeons assisted by artisans, such as jewelers or *woodworkers.*

During the Middle Ages, dental practice was almost entirely in the hands of barber-surgeons, as was all surgery in Europe after the 12th century, when priests and monks—as most were physicians then—were forbidden by the church to perform any surgical procedures. Although some barber-surgeons became

This German dentist is described in the accompanying verse as pulling teeth painlessly "as one bears children." In the upper left-hand corner is a string of teeth, an advertisement for his trade. (By Jost Amman, from The Book of Trades, *late 16th century)*

skilled dental practitioners, the majority deserved their low reputation as "tooth-pullers," that being the most common dental treatment. Their bloody reputation may also be related to the fact that teeth were pulled as a form of punishment in the Middle Ages, for such crimes as eating meat during Lent or failing to pay required sums to one's lord. "Tooth-drawers," then, were seen as little better than executioners. Arab dental workers were the exception. Because they preferred not to draw blood, they pulled teeth only when absolutely necessary. But, if a tooth had to be pulled, the barber who yanked it out swiftly was often preferred to the physician who, following accepted medical practice, would agonizingly loosen the tooth, sometimes for hours, before pulling it.

In the 14th century, barber-surgeons, like other

tradespeople, began to form guilds, which included both men and women. These guilds set standards for their many duties, including dental operations, and they licensed barber-surgeons within the guild area. Gradually, as private, non-church universities came into being and some surgeons began to have academic training, the mostly illiterate barbers and the educated surgeons began to diverge. A 14th-century French surgeon, Guy de Chauliac, recommended that dentistry be made part of the medical profession and practiced by trained surgeons. But his advice went unheeded for another four centuries. In practice, trained surgeons primarily treated the wealthy classes, while barbers still used their old-fashioned skills on poorer people. Both groups still believed worms were the cause of many dental problems. This belief was not questioned in print until the mid-1500s and was still being seriously discussed two centuries later.

The first books specifically on dentistry were published in Europe in the 16th century. Dentists first became distinguished as medical specialists in France, which was in the forefront of surgical practice at the time. In the early part of the 17th century, the term *chirurgien dentiste* (*surgeon-dentist*), came into use as a separate title. From 1697 on, an aspiring surgeon-dentist in France was required to attend the College of Surgeons, work two years with a licensed dentist, pass a set examination on theory and practice, and take an oath of ethics before being certified as an *expert pour les dents*.

Pierre Fauchard, widely regarded as the father of modern dentistry, published a classic work, *Le Chirurgien Dentiste*, in 1728. Fauchard stated clearly for the first time that dental decay was *not* caused by worms. At a time when medical practitioners kept their techniques and formulas secret—to keep their "competitive edge" and to maintain an aura of mystery—Fauchard helped establish the principle that dental techniques should be shared for the improvement of dentistry in general.

The French set a model for their counterparts in Europe and elsewhere, and surgeon-dentists gradually came to be the only practitioners licensed to practice dentistry. Although not allowed to study medicine at universities, women were initially allowed to study and practice dentistry in France. After the 1740s, however, dentistry was restricted to men.

In colonial or frontier areas and in some rural parts of Europe, dentistry continued to be practiced by anyone who could pick up the skills, including *barbers, pharmacists, blacksmiths, jewelers, silversmiths,* as well as traveling charlatans of all kinds. The famous Boston silversmith Paul Revere, for example, advertised that he "fixed teeth" on the side. Indeed, one of France's contributions to America during the Revolutionary War was to send two dentists, Joseph Le Mayeur and James Gardette. These men taught their skills to others in America, helping found the profession of dentistry on the new continent. One of their pupils, John Greenwood, developed the first foot-powered dental drill and later provided George Washington with his sets of false teeth.

Many religious Americans were opposed to pulling teeth, claiming that, since teeth were given by the Creator, they should be kept except in cases of extreme pain. While that might be an understandable reaction to the eager tooth-pullers of the time, it meant that many people were chronically ill and even died because they had severely diseased teeth. The early American physician Benjamin Rush helped change that thinking when he cured several invalids of "chronic rheumatism" by removing their diseased teeth.

The lead in dental practice gradually passed from Europe to America. The first independent dental school was founded in 1840 in Baltimore, Maryland, after the founders failed to convince the local medical school to add a dental curriculum; only a year before that the first dental journal and the first dental association were founded, both also in the United States. In the same period, various states began to license dentists, the first being Alabama in 1841. Europe followed suit, with the first separate dental schools being founded in England in 1858-59.

Some trained dental professionals established clinics for the poor—as early as 1791 in New York City and throughout the 1800s elsewhere in America and Europe. These clinics, largely supported by the dentists, provided practical experience for student dentists and also began to create a public demand for professional dental care. This was especially important in North America, where there was little call for trained dentists until after the Civil War. Although education and licensing standards had been established in many states by then, vast rural and frontier areas still supported many charlatans and experienced but untrained tooth-drawers. In 1870, only 10 percent of the 10,000 dentists in the United States were school-trained. It is no wonder that the Canadian Province of Ontario in 1868 found it necessary to pass an act requiring that, in order to be registered, any dentist must first have five years of resident practice in a Canadian dental office—a law aimed at stopping the flow of untrained, self-proclaimed dentists from south of the border.

Dentists themselves had to struggle to upgrade their trade to a profession. While dentists in Europe were considered part of the educated class, surgery in general still had considerably lower status than it has today. In the United States, the earliest trained dentists were interested primarily in the mechanical aspects of dental surgery. They had to be compelled to attend the other courses of study, such as physiology and chemistry, that are involved in dentistry. Indeed, the 19th century saw many important technical advances in the field of dentistry, among them the first dental chair, the first electric dental drill, and—as important in dentistry as in other fields of surgery—the development of anesthetics. All these advances made more dental training necessary. The field gradually moved towards its modern professional qualification requirements—a

Like most surgeons for many centuries, this 16th-century chirurgien-dentist is operating out of an open shop in a public square, serving as something of a medical sideshow. (By Lucas Van Leyden, Rijksmuseum, Amsterdam)

scientifically oriented pre-dental college education of several years, depending on the country, followed by graduation from a dental school granting a D.D.S. (Doctor of Dental Surgery) or a D.D.M. (Doctor of Dental

Medicine), and passage of an examination for a license to practice.

As professional training and public demand increased, dentists in permanent offices became the norm. Traveling dental mechanics gradually disappeared in most developed countries, although they are still found in other parts of the world. In 1891, the United States Government changed the census classification for dentist from technician to professional, which signaled a significant change in the status of dentists, which today is nearly equal to that of physicians.

With scientific and technical innovations came a shift in emphasis in dental practice. Better understanding of the causes of tooth decay led dentists to focus more on preventive hygiene; the introduction of X-ray machines led to earlier diagnoses of problems; the development of many new techniques allowed greater success in preserving natural teeth. Dentists are general practitioners, all licensed to carry out virtually the full range of dental operations, if necessary. However, with the increasing range of techniques involved, some dentists in populated areas have chosen to specialize, which often involves postgraduate training. In the United States, for example, approximately 10 percent of all dentists are specialists.

Orthodontists are perhaps the best known of the dental specialists, especially in the United States, where they formed their first association in 1900. Although orthodontics had been attempted since Egyptian times, only in the 20th century has the use of bands and appliances to straighten teeth become a practical reality. *Oral surgeons,* many of whom are also physicians, carry out corrective surgery of the mouth and jaw area, often in hospitals, while *oral pathologists* specialize in diagnosing tumors or diseases of the mouth. *Endodontists* specialize in treating interior dental structures, carrying out procedures such as root canal surgery.

Pedodontists focus on the dental needs and fears of children. This specialty has gained in importance in the

20th century because it stresses the early education of and preventive dental care for children and adolescents.

Prosthodontists are dental specialists who create false teeth and other replacement reconstructions for the mouth and jaw. Although people had tried for centuries to create dental replacements, prosthesis did not become practical until Philip Pfaff, dentist to the Prussian King Frederick the Great, developed the technique of using plaster models from wax impressions, a process made public in 1755. The development of porcelain teeth by the French chemist Duchâteau in 1774 and the production of Vulcanite in 1855 by the American Charles Goodyear allowed further advances in prosthodontics. In creating early dental prostheses, dentists at first had to rely on whatever skilled artisans were available, often jewelers, woodworkers, and ivory carvers. Gradually, however, there developed a group of specially trained people called *dental laboratory technicians* or *dental mechanics,* who today construct dental appliances such as crowns, bridges, and dentures according to the dentist's specifications. These technicians usually work in laboratories; some are employed by private dental offices but are not allowed to work directly with patients.

Other auxiliary dental occupations have also developed in the last century. *Dental hygienists* have been taking over many of the cleaning, X-raying, and instructional functions in dental offices since 1905, when a Connecticut dentist first trained his assistant to perform some of these procedures and later founded a dental hygienists' school. Dental hygienists, who are often women, generally must have two to four years of college and special training in a dental hygiene school, and must pass a licensing examination. Some other countries, such as the United Kingdom and New Zealand, have similar requirements for what they call *dental nurses* or *dental auxiliaries*. In the Soviet Union, people carrying out those functions are called "two-year dentists," with "three-year dentists" being the equivalent of the general dental practitioner and "five-year dentists" being specialists called *stomatologists* (*stomato* is the Greek word for mouth). Many countries also employ *dental assistants* who often have had some training beyond high school. They handle record keeping, clean instruments, and assist the dentist, but they do not work directly with the patients.

Most dentists work in private offices which were, around the turn of the century, called dental parlors. But in some places dentists have formed group practices. Many dentists and dental specialists are employed by large institutions, including the military services. *Oral pathologists* are generally employed by dental schools or universities, and *public health dentists,* who specialize in public education regarding dental health, are employed by government or private agencies. In countries like the Soviet Union, all dentists are employed by the government. *Forensic odontologists,* who specialize in identifying bodies based on dental remains and dental records, are employed by investigative or legal agencies.

Except for a few decades in France in the mid-1700s, women were barred from dentistry by being barred from university training. As they moved into other academic areas in the 19th century, however, they also began to move into dentistry. The first woman graduate of a dental school in the United States was Lucy Hobbs, who graduated from the Ohio College of Dental Surgery in 1866. As in other medical specialties, women were often partners with their husbands. The first woman dentist to maintain her own dental office in the United States, for example, was Emmeline Roberts Jones, who practiced with her husband and then continued the practice on her own after his death in 1864.

More recent developments, such as high-speed drills, antibiotics, and sophisticated anesthetics, have made dentists even more efficient at preserving and maintaining their patients' teeth. Some have even become cosmetic specialists, fashioning crowns for the teeth of public figures whose smiles are their fortunes. Dental work can be expensive, but it has become recognized as so vital that

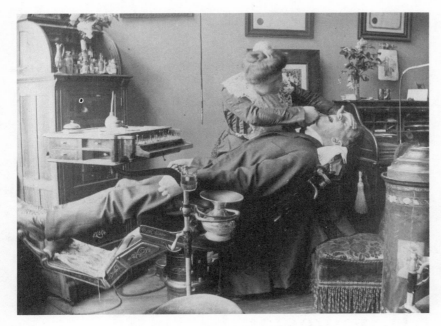

By the time Dr. Olga Lentz was operating as a dentist in early 20th-century Minnesota, dental operations had moved into private offices with recognizable specialized chairs and equipment. (Photo by Albert Munson, Minnesota Historical Society)

many health insurance plans cover necessary dental care. As with all medical specialties, dentists are concentrated in populated areas in developed countries, with rural areas being less well provided for, and with undeveloped countries making do with little or no dental care. Modern international social agencies, however, are attempting to introduce modern dentistry to places where traveling barber-surgeons still operate.

For related occupations in this volume, *Healers,* see the following:
    Barbers
    Nurses
    Pharmacists
    Physicians and Surgeons
    Veterinarians

For related occupations in other volumes of the series, see the following:
in *Artists and Artisans:*
    Jewelers

Midwives and Obstetricians

For thousands of years, *midwives* delivered almost all human beings. Generally a midwife was an older woman (in a very few societies, an old man) who made a specialty of attending mothers in childbirth. The Latin word *obstetrix,* in fact, means "she who is present." In early cultures, and in some modern so-called primitive societies, the mother often delivered her child while sitting on the lap of the midwife, who sat with legs wide apart. This position allowed the midwife to knead, push, and prod the mother's belly, attempting to hasten the birth of the child. By Biblical times in Egypt and Mesopotamia, this position had given way to the use of a birthing stool or obstetrical chair—a semicircular chair open in the middle—on which the mother sat to deliver her child. The use of this chair was so widespread, and the midwife's services so routine at every birth, that when the Egyptian Pharaoh (in Exodus 1:16) wanted to kill off all the newborn male children of the Jews, he commanded the midwives: "When you do the office of midwife to the Hebrew women, and see them upon the birthstool, if it is a son, you shall kill him." (The midwives disobeyed, following a strong rule not to kill the infants they delivered.) While some peoples used special couches or piles of bricks placed in a semicircle, most midwives carried an obstetrical chair with them as standard equipment into the 17th century, and in some places even later.

While a woman was in labor, midwives would sing sacred songs to ease the pain and speed delivery. Midwives used various methods to hasten delivery: they picked up the woman and dropped her, or tied her to a couch and shook it, hoping to jar the child loose; they tied the woman to a tree and had someone drive straight at

For thousands of years, most women gave birth in a seated position, often on a stool or on a pile of bricks, like this woman in delivery, attended by midwives. (Bibliothèque Nationale, Paris, Ms. arabe 5847, fol. 122v.)

her on a horse, veering away only at the last minute, hoping to frighten the child from her womb; or they had the mother stand with legs apart over a fire, hoping the warmth would cause the child to emerge. Requirements for being a midwife were minimal. A book of writings by the early Indian physician Susruta notes only that a woman giving birth should be attended by four aged and knowing women whose nails were well-trimmed. Such specifications stood for thousands of years. Other common requirements were good character, honesty, and small hands. Most cultures also required that a prospective midwife should have borne at least one child herself.

Midwives were very much on their own, with little access to medical advice or training. In early Greece, pregnant women were not allowed into the temples of healing where most medical care was provided. And throughout much of history male physicians were, for reasons of modesty, allowed to examine women patients only in extreme cases. While midwives were mostly from the lower classes, many were highly respected for their skill—among them the mother of the philosopher Socrates—and were called upon by upper-class women.

In Greece and some other places, there developed two classes of midwives. The first were the regular midwives, who often operated in teams of four or more, headed by an experienced chief midwife. The second were the *medical midwives* who were called in to help in difficult cases; they could give drugs to hasten delivery or ease pain. Only in extremely important or problematic cases would a male physician be called in. One major exception to this was in India, where male physicians generally delivered children from upper-caste women in order to prevent their contamination from contact with lower castes. After a birth, the midwife often stayed with the mother and child, sometimes for as long as a month, advising on diet and also recommending a *wet nurse* for the child.

Greek midwives, possibly with the help of male physicians, did make one extraordinarily valuable advance: they developed the technique of *podalic version* (turning by the feet), known to only a few other cultures until Renaissance times. When the child was cross-wise or feet-down in the womb, the midwife would reach into the womb, grasp the infant's foot and (where possible) turn the body into a head-down position so it could be delivered normally. This technique—which seems so obvious to us today—saved the lives of thousands of women and children. After the child was born, the midwife cut the umbilical cord, disposed of the afterbirth, and took the child to the father. In Greece, the father would lift the child into the air to acknowledge his acceptance of the child as his own. However, if the parents rejected the child, the midwife was supposed to "expose" the child in the open, often near a temple, leaving it to die or be adopted by a passerby. This was often done if the child was weak or deformed, or if its father was unknown. In a few cultures, some female infants were drowned.

If the best efforts of the midwife or physician failed to bring about delivery, either the mother or child (or both) died. If the child died in the womb but the mother lived, the midwife would call in a *barber-surgeon, shepherd, hog-gelder,* or anyone strong and skilled with a knife, to carry out the "child-breaking" operation. The child was hacked to pieces in the mother's womb and removed piecemeal, using the hooks and forceps that hung on the midwife's belt, also symbols of her trade. In Greece, the killing of the child was sometimes permitted, to save the life of the mother. In cases where the mother died first, the child would be cut from her womb. This procedure was called a Caesarean section, probably because the laws regulating it were part of the *Lex Cesare.* Julius Caesar was probably *not* born this way, since the operation on live women was almost always fatal and Caesar's mother lived for many years after his birth.

Midwives had other responsibilities, too. They were called in to examine young women, to certify their virginity and assess their probable child-bearing ability. As a result, many midwives throughout history worked also as *matchmakers.* In some countries, especially in later Islamic countries, midwives were employed to cut away parts of a young girl's genital organs. Some midwives even specialized in this practice, becoming traveling female *circumcisers*. Midwives were also called in to determine when a pregnancy existed, and to predict the sex and birth date of the child. In addition, many midwives served as *abortionists* (and in Rome sometimes as professional *poisoners*). In Greece and other pre-Christian civilizations, abortions were legally permitted and quite commonly performed by midwives.

In many cultures midwives, especially the senior medical midwives, also acted as general practitioners for women, dealing not only with birth but also with specific female ailments and common illnesses. In this they had some help from the male physicians. Although questions of modesty and the low status of women often prevented physicians from treating female patients directly, some physicians throughout history tried to raise the level of medical care for women. As early as Egyptian times, medical writings included prescriptions to ease obstetrical and gynecological problems. Soranus, a Greek

In China a midwife would stay with a mother and newborn child for as long as a month. This mother is supporting her nursing baby in the angle of her raised leg. (Courtesy of the Wellcome Trustees)

physician from Ephesus, gathered knowledge about such subjects in a book published for midwives in 100 A.D. In Classical times, Greek physicians and midwives developed some of the basic tools and techniques for gynecological examinations.

But in the fourth century, Rome adopted Christianity and medicine fell into disfavor. Medical institutions and records were destroyed as "pagan." Physicians and midwives continued for some time to pass on their knowledge and experience to their apprentices, but when the Western Roman Empire fell two centuries later, these social patterns of transmission were disrupted. In the turbulent period that followed, medicines and techniques were lost or distorted. Most important for midwifery, knowledge of the important podalic version techniques gradually died out altogether. For the next thousand years, until the technique was rediscovered in the 16th century, thousands of women and infants needlessly lost their lives.

The Middle Ages were indeed dark ones for midwifery. Where Greek science had once made some progress toward rational medicine, ignorance and superstition prevailed. As the church now entered the childbirth process, salvation of the child's soul was considered most important, even at the expense of the mother's life. At times the church decreed that in difficult deliveries where the child's life was at hazard, an unborn child must be cut from its mother's womb, in order to be baptized. This meant almost certain death for the mother, in those days when abdominal surgery was otherwise unknown. Midwives generally refused to carry out this Caesarean operation, preferring to save the mother and let the child die in the womb, if necessary. For this refusal, some people charged midwives with being in league with the devil. In later periods, as in 16th-century England, midwives were trained to perform baptisms themselves, in cases where ordained church officials could not be summoned in time.

Like their contemporaries, most medieval midwives

were ignorant and superstitious. When called out at night, midwives would often travel in pairs, so as not to be caught alone with the Devil. Midwives continued to use non-Christian drugs, charms, amulets, and invocations in the course of their work. This laid them open to charges that they had sold a child's soul to the devil or deliberately killed an infant at the devil's behest. Many midwives supplemented their small incomes by fortune-telling, preparing love potions, and performing other secret services believed to be in their special power. The status of midwives in this period was extremely low. In some parts of Europe, they were considered even more despicable than *barbers* or *executioners,* and midwives' sons were barred from some trade guilds. While *nurses* of the period were high-born, well-educated women working in convent hospices (the forerunners of today's hospitals), midwives were mostly illiterate and drawn from the lower classes.

In the Middle Ages, men—and their more current medical knowledge—were almost completely barred from the childbirth process. In Europe astrologers would sometimes be brought into the lying-in room in order to cast the infant's horoscope at the precise moment of birth. But in the Islamic world even that contact was forbidden, so segregated were women and men. Moslem women patients and midwives could consult with male physicians only through a heavy curtain; they had no direct access to medical knowledge. Zealous concern for modesty was also the rule in Europe. Even the midwife worked by touch under the skirts of the mother in delivery, never seeing the parts of the body she was working with.

As medicine began to revive, however, some male physicians began once again to concern themselves with the medical care of women. Some of the works of Soranus reached Europe from the Islamic world, where Greek texts had been translated and annotated. These were circulated through the medical schools that were being established. In the earliest of the medical schools at

During the Middle Ages, the only men allowed into the delivery room, besides occasional knife-wielders, were astrologers, like those at the window here preparing the horoscope of the child about to be born. (By Jost Amman, from De Generatione Hominis)

Salerno in the ninth century, some women were admitted; one, popularly called Dame Trotula, may have written an early text for midwives. Medical training was soon foreclosed to women again, but these works did provide the basis for new efforts to instruct midwives in aiding women in childbirth. One such book was *The Garden of Roses for Pregnant Women and for Midwives*, published in 1513 but based on Soranus's work from over 1,400 years before. Attempts by male barber-surgeons to gain direct access to women in labor sometimes had disastrous results. Dr. Wertt, a Hamburg physician, dressed as a female midwife in order to do so, and for his transgression he was burned alive at the stake in 1522. Attempts throughout Europe to raise the level of midwifery led to licensing of midwives by their municipalities, generally after examination by an appointed city physician.

But religious hysteria persisted in Europe. From the 15th through 18th centuries, tens of thousands of people were executed as witches, and many others were charged with witchcraft. A great number of these women were midwives. So strong was the association between the two in the popular mind that a 1595 textbook on midwifery flatly stated that many midwives were indeed witches.

But in the meantime, knowledge of obstetrics and gynecology was beginning to grow again. Although few midwives could read, some of the knowledge collected in midwifery textbooks filtered down to them. As surgeons began to separate themselves from barbers, Ambroise Paré—son of a barber and often called the father of modern surgery—established a school for midwives in Paris, setting the model for others elsewhere in Europe. These midwifery schools attracted women of some education and social class, like Louise Bourgeois. She had graduated from the Hôtel Dieu (House of God), a hospital in Paris. She later became the "sworn midwife" of Paris and officiated at royal births. But just as midwives were becoming better trained and more effective, male surgeons—who had learned the technique of podalic version—began to come into the birth process. The traveling knife-wielders who had for centuries been called in to assist midwives in dismembering unborn dead children were barred from the "child-breaking" process. Instead, surgeons were called in. As they developed new techniques for saving mother and child in difficult deliveries, they began to convert what would formerly have been child-death situations into successful childbirths. Autopsies being allowed for the first time in many centuries, surgeons like Fallopius were discovering the internal parts of the female anatomy.

Midwives protested vigorously against the intrusion of men into their domain, and their claims of modesty and tradition were supported by the church and by many women. Nevertheless men moved steadily into the field of childbirth—and two occupations developed, sharply divided by sex and class. Serving the poorer people were midwives, most of whom had no access to medical training nor necessarily any desire for learning from men, whom they regarded as intruders. Attending wealthy and fashionable women were male midwives. These *man midwives* were especially common in France, which led the way in trained midwifery and obstetric surgery. Male midwives began to replace the old midwives' birthing stool with delivery on a bed. They soon became fashionable among the French nobility and in 1670 a male midwife, Julien Clement, attended the queen of France in childbirth. To separate themselves from female midwives, Clement and other male practitioners in France adopted the title *accoucheur,* the French word for bed being *couche.* Use of the bed did not allow *accoucheurs* to see more of the birth process themselves, however, for the birth generally took place under cover—as it had with female midwives before them. Sometimes the ends of a sheet were tied around the necks of the mother and *accoucheur,* respectively. Occasionally the male midwife was even blindfolded.

The other major innovation in midwifery in the 16th century was developed by the infamous Chamberlen (sometimes Anglicized as Chamberlain) family, French barber-surgeons who settled in England. Peter Chamberlen developed the obstetrical forceps, a tool with two scoop-like arms that could be used to grasp a child by the head and pull it from the womb. The Chamberlens were able to keep this invention a secret for over a century, while enhancing their family fortune. Not until 1721 were obstetrical forceps developed independently. Their inventor, Jean Palfyne, a Belgian, quickly made his tool available to others, through the Paris Academy.

Male midwives were still subject to public abuse for

their work, especially from the female midwives with whom they competed. Dr. William Smellie, who established a school for midwives in London in the 18th century, was attacked by a female competitor as "a great-horse-godmother of a he-midwife." Like the French, the English male midwives adopted their own term, to separate themselves from the untrained female midwives; they called themselves *obstetricians*. Questions of modesty continued to be raised, especially in Victorian England, and operating under a sheet continued to be the pattern. In fact, blind obstetricians—like one highly successful practitioner in Philadelphia—were praised as the ultimate in modesty for women in delivery. Female midwives continued to deliver most children, and sometimes acted as assistants for trained *accoucheurs* and obstetricians. Some also continued to perform abortions, although that was not only illegal, but even a capital offense in some parts of Europe.

Along with other European settlers, midwives moved to colonies around the world. The first midwife in what would become the United States, for example, came over with her husband, Dr. Samuel Fuller, on the *Mayflower*. The second was Anne Hutchinson, later expelled from the Massachusetts Bay Colony for her religious beliefs. Not all colonial midwives were women, as this notice from the *New York Weekly Post Boy* of July 22, 1745, indicates: "Last night died in the Prime of Life, to the almost universal Regret and Sorrow of this City, Mr. John Dupuy, M.D., Man Mid-wife . . . there is none like him."

In the 18th and 19th centuries, the role of the midwife decreased sharply, as questions of modesty gave way to questions of training. Many obstetricians were trained physicians or surgeons who took special obstetrical training. Even those men who took brief obstetrics courses had more training than most female midwives, who were generally barred from university training. The first department of obstetrics was established at the University of Glasgow in 1739, and its graduates spread such specialized training out around the world. Use of

This version of the birth of the Virgin Mary gives a picture of a delivery room in 16th-century Germany, with midwives and assistants resting and refreshing themselves. Note the implements hanging from the belt of the senior midwife in the front. (By Albrecht Dürer, from The Life of the Virgin)

forceps and other such instruments was generally restricted to physicians, so women in labor more often began to call obstetricians, rather than the midwives. Branded as old-fashioned, the obstetrical chair—part of the standard equipment of child delivery for thousands

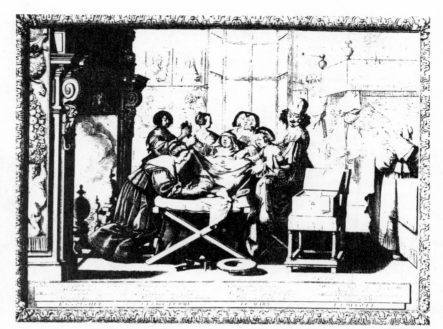

By the time of this 17th-century childbirth, French midwives had begun to substitute beds for birthing stools and husbands like this one were occasionally allowed to attend the birth.
(L'Accouchement, *by Abraham Bosse, reproduced from* Medicine and the Artist [Ars Medica] *by permission of the Philadelphia Museum of Art)*

of years—was gradually abandoned, as female midwives followed the male practice of delivery in bed.

The use of modern techniques was not always welcomed, however. Obstetrics, since Paré in the 16th century, had been regarded as a branch of surgery, and the introduction of forceps had led to a heavy use—some said an overuse—of mechanical aids in deliveries. A conservative reaction set in, sparked especially in England by another Glasgow graduate, Dr. William Hunter, who promoted natural childbirth.

During these same centuries, women began to turn to physicians rather than midwives for diagnosis and treatment of their sexual ailments. Physicians specializing in these areas came to be known as *gynecologists*. Initially they were hampered by excessive modesty regarding contacts between male physicians and female patients, by inadequate knowledge of anatomy and physiology, and by the great dangers that attended any operations in the days before anesthetics and disinfectants. But by the early 19th century, physicians working under emergency conditions on the American frontier pioneered some gynecological operations, which laid the foundation for future medical advances. In Kentucky in 1809, Edinburgh-trained Dr. Ephraim McDowell carried out the first successful operation to remove ovarian cysts from a woman.

There still remained, however, the problems of pain and infection. While some 19th-century practitioners were beginning to experiment with hypnotism as a means of avoiding pain, they were almost universally branded charlatans (as some of them surely were). In any case, their hypnotism was soon laid aside with the discovery of anesthetics, including ether, nitrous oxide gas (laughing gas), and chloroform. The first "painless childbirth" occurred in 1847. While many religious leaders insisted that the Bible stated that women should bring forth children in pain, such tongues were silenced when Queen Victoria in 1853 gave birth to Prince Leopold under chloroform. From this point on, where physicians were available and women could afford their fees, obstetricians were widely preferred. Midwives were generally confined to delivering children in the poor and rural parts of the world. Anesthetics also made possible a wide range of abdominal operations that, before then, had been performed only in life-and-death situations because of the pain and hazards involved.

Such operations and deliveries, however, could not fulfill their promise until physicians better understood how disease spread through human contact. As urban populations increased and many deliveries took place in maternity hospitals or wards, the major hazard of childbirth was no longer inability to deliver the child, but childbed fever, also called puerperal fever. In 1843 American physician and writer Oliver Wendell Holmes stated that childbed fever—which killed as many as one-third of all mothers in the major urban hospitals of North America and Europe—was a contagious disease spread from patient to patient by physicians, midwives, and other attendants. He was ridiculed for suggesting that a "gentleman" could carry disease. In the same decade, but independently, Viennese physician Ignaz Semmelweiss noticed that in the lying-in hospital where he served, mortality of mothers in the ward served by medical students was five times greater than that of mothers in the ward served by midwives. He soon found that, while waiting for a woman in labor, students would often work in the dissection room, to which all the hospital's corpses were sent, regardless of the cause of death and without being embalmed in antiseptic. Following the practice of the times, students did not wash their hands when going from the dissection room to the maternity ward, nor indeed did physicians or midwives wash their hands between examinations of different women.

Unfortunately, when Semmelweiss tried to introduce disinfection for students and midwives, as well as more hygienic hospital procedures in general, he was subjected to abuse and, successively, loss of his job, his reputation, and his sanity. His position was not eased by his habit of calling hospital personnel "murderers" whenever a woman died of childbed fever. Like Holmes, Semmelweiss saw his theory buried under a weight of habit and ignorance. But unlike Holmes, he took to the streets pasting up placards stating: "Fathers, do you know what it means when you call a doctor or a midwife to the bed of your wife in labour? You are summoning death into your house. A death which is so easy to banish by [my] method. . . . " Semmelweiss himself died in 1865, ironically of childbed fever contracted through a scratch while he delivered a baby. Disinfection and hygienic methods of delivery were not adopted by doctors or midwives until the work of Joseph Lister later in that decade.

Thereafter, the balance between midwife and obstetrician developed very differently in the United States than in Europe. In the United States, obstetricians—almost all male—established a virtual monopoly on delivery of children. Their advantages were great. They had medical training, still foreclosed to all but the most exceptional and determined women; they had the ability to operate and to administer anesthetics; and, as hospitals became the main centers for dispensing medical care and doctors came to control them, they were able to withhold hospital privileges from midwives. By the 1920s, obstetricians delivered 80 percent of the children born in the United States. That figure would have been higher but for the midwives who accompanied the millions of immigrants from southern and eastern Europe in the early 20th century. Midwives with no formal training continued to operate only where doctors were scarce or unwilling to serve, such as in rural areas or in poor or immigrant communities in large cities.

In Western Europe, obstetrical care was more conservative than in the United States. Following the lead of Dr. William Hunter, many European obstetricians were less eager to use forceps, Caesarean sections, and anesthetics than their American colleagues were. In addition, as trained nurses came to be standard, midwifery in Europe was largely transformed from a lay occupation into a highly skilled nursing specialty. *Nurse-midwives* attended the majority of normal births in many countries in Europe, with obstetricians called in only in cases of difficulty. In the 1920s, for example, 80 percent of Swedish births were attended by trained midwives.

Social reformers in the early 20th century, seeing the need for trained midwives in poor, immigrant, and rural communities in the United States, encouraged women to obtain nurse-midwife training in Europe and return to help train others. Their numbers were always small, however, and in the years after World War II, some states stopped licensing midwives. Lay midwives then almost disappeared in the United States. Reliance on nurse-midwives in Europe also diminished somewhat during this period.

The 1960s and 1970s witnessed a negative reaction by many women to what they saw as excessive mechanical interference in the birth process by obstetricians working in impersonal hospitals. They pointed out that the infant and maternal mortality rate was relatively high in the

United States, where these practices were most widespread, as compared to other industrialized countries. This led to a revival of interest in natural childbirth, in which drugs and instruments are used only when necessary. This revival led, in turn, to a resurgence of midwifery and childbirth at home, in industrialized countries where those practices had become largely things of the past. However, many obstetricians have charged that such conditions are not properly germ-free and provide insufficient emergency medical help. Whatever its value in urban areas, the European nurse-midwife model is especially well-suited to developing countries and remote areas where physicians are scarce. This model has been spread widely by the World Health Organization (WHO), with trained midwives gradually replacing the remaining lay midwives in most countries.

In recent decades, as many more women have obtained medical training, an increasing number are choosing to specialize in obstetrics and gynecology. And as nursing and nurse-midwifery have come to be respected trained specialties, men as well as women have been moving into these occupations, notably in northern Europe. Ironically, some of these men have faced the same kind of criticism and discrimination faced by the earliest "man midwives." Clearly, the ways in which obstetricians and midwives work together in the childbirth process are varied and still changing, but it is possible that—at some time in the future—attendance at childbirth will no longer be sex-typed work.

For related occupations in this volume, *Healers,* see the following:
    Barbers
    Nurses
    Pharmacists
    Physicians and Surgeons

For related occupations in other volumes of the series, see the following:
in *Helpers and Aides:*
  Child Nurses
  Matchmakers
in *Restaurateurs and Innkeepers:*
  Prostitutes
in *Scholars and Priests:*
  Priests
in *Scientists and Technologists:*
  Astrologers

Nurses

The profession of nursing has had a long, slow development, often sharply affected by social and religious changes, and tied to the emergence of a hospital system. Early societies had no communal arrangements for long-term patient care; the sick were cared for at home by family members or *servants* who prepared and administered home remedies. Such caretakers were untrained and often—especially in the case of *slaves*—unmotivated, but this pattern of home nursing was dominant for thousands of years in many parts of the world, persisting even into the 20th century in some places. Nursing as an occupation did not emerge until the rise of communal health care.

The earliest centers of healing, the "temples of sleep" in early Egypt and Greece, did not have *nurses* as such. These centers were religious as much as medical, and

This scene from an Asclepian temple shows a priest-physician treating a patient on the left and a nursing assistant on the right tending another patient in "incubation," or recuperative sleep. (National Archaeological Museum, Athens)

were designed for brief visits; they did not accept seriously ill, pregnant, or long-term patients. In the Asclepian temples of sleep of Greece (named after the priest-physician-god Asclepius), men and women patients slept in different areas and seem to have been served by male and female attendants respectively. Among the attendants who reported to the chief priest were two sets of priestesses, one of whom assisted in the "holy mysteries." The other was called the "basket-bearer," possibly the equivalent of a head nurse, who carried out practical duties for the care of the sick and supervised the *bath attendants* and other helpers who fed, washed, or carried the infirm.

The earliest trained nurses were young men, often apprentice physicians. Hippocrates, the great Greek physician who lived and worked in the fifth century B.C., despaired of using untrained servants to care for patients. Instead he placed students by his patients' bedsides, to carry out his prescriptions and to observe and learn from the progress of the disease. But Hippocrates' influence was greater in history than in his own time, and this practice was not widely followed by other healers for centuries.

Not until the third century B.C., when hospitals began to be established in India, did a class of trained nurses first come into existence. The early Indian medical writer, Susruta, showed clearly that nursing was a distinct and honored occupation, noting: "The physician, the patient, the drug, and the nurse are the four feet of medicine upon which the cure depends." These nurses were mostly young men from the Brahmins, the priestly order; some were elderly women trained to wait upon women patients, since men were not allowed to do so. According to Indian medical writings, the nurse had to know how to compound drugs and be

> . . . skilled in every kind of service that a patient may require, endowed with general cleverness, competent to cook food, skilled in bathing or washing the patient, well conversant with rubbing and massaging the limbs, lifting the patient or assisting him to walk about, well skilled in making or cleaning beds, ready, patient, and skillful in waiting upon one who is ailing, and never unwilling to do anything that may be ordered.

While Brahmin nurses normally cared for patients of their own caste, Buddhist reformers laid aside questions of caste, urging that care be provided for all. Indians built a vast chain of clean, well-constructed hospitals in response to Buddhist teachings of compassion, mercy, and justice. Like hospitals everywhere until the late 19th century, these were intended for the poor, the rich being treated at home. Indian hospitals stressed prevention as well as cure. Hygiene and sanitation were given great attention, even being made part of religious observances, and *musicians* and *storytellers* were employed to cheer the hospital patients. Here nursing achieved its highest level in the ancient world. After the eighth century A.D., however, nursing in India went into decline, along with medical care and Buddhism in general.

While early India had an elaborate medical system, the Romans of the time had virtually none. Before Greek medicine was imported to Italy in the third century B.C., the Romans did not even have professional physicians, much less nurses. Nursing was done at home by family or slaves. Sick and wounded *soldiers* tended each other using crude first aid and, if necessary, were placed in private homes for recuperation. As the Roman armies spread farther from home, however, portable tent hospitals and then permanent hospitals were established at key points around the empire. These permanent hospitals were set up on a well-designed corridor system, with wards built for five to six patients each. Baths, recreation areas, and pharmacies were available for all. The medical staff—one *physician/surgeon* and a body of male nursing attendants for each legion of 5,000 men—had their own rooms at these hospitals. The nursing attendants had no formal training, their main duty being to tend to the needs of recuperating patients. One group of Roman military nurses were, in fact, simply called *contubernalis* (tent companions).

As medical care became more widespread, some non-military hospitals also developed in the Roman Empire around this time. Hospitals called *valetudinaria* were set up on large estates for treating ill slaves, who were, after all, valuable property. In addition, some physicians started small private hospitals called *iatreia,* which were connected to the Asclepian temples. Patients recuperating from operations or being kept under observation were attended in the *iatreia* by physicians, students, and slaves, who seem to have done the actual nursing.

By the second and third centuries A.D., Romans had generally recognized the need for a group of people to perform nursing functions. But no specialized training was thought necessary and the work was still most often carried out by slaves under medical or military supervision. Although a professional class of trained nurses might well have developed from this base, the course of nursing was abruptly diverted when Rome adopted Christianity as the state religion. In 335 A.D., Emperor Constantine ordered the closing of all pagan institutions, including the Asclepian temples and most other medical schools and institutions. With them passed much of the medical skill and learning of the ancient world. Apart from its pagan associations, Greek and Roman medicine fell into disgrace because the early Christians—much like modern faith healers—believed cures could come only through religious means, not medical.

Although they rejected medicine, the Christians put into practice their ideas of charity, which set nursing on a very different path. Christian *bishops* were charged with the care of the sick, poor, widowed, orphaned, and disabled, as well as providing hospitality for strangers traveling in their area. The bishops, in turn, delegated care of these people to a group of church officials called *deacons* and *deaconesses*. They and many other affluent Christians set up a special room, called a *diakonus* (literally a Christ-room), in their homes for those who needed aid. Deaconesses also visited the sick and poor at home, bringing food and providing watchful nursing care. This laid the basis for the development of not only nursing, but social work as well.

By the late fourth century, Christians were establishing public institutions to provide care for the sick and needy. Such institutions went under a variety of names but gradually came to be known as *hospices*. Some structures were newly built and staffed by wealthy Christians; other hospices were founded on the sites of old Asclepian temples. The word *hospice* itself comes from the Latin *hospitum,* meaning hospitality (the word *hospital* came later). Such an institution was also called a *Hôtel Dieu* or *Maison Dieu* (House of God). These institutions were regarded as shelters for those who could not care for themselves, less like a modern hospital than a combination nursing home, orphanage, old-age home, and traveler's-aid shelter. In early Christian times, no physicians or surgeons were associated with such hospices. The nursing staff—mostly wealthy Christian volunteers—provided for patients' most basic physical needs, and focused on religious practices rather than on medical attention.

The Middle Ages

As the Roman Empire fell apart in the fifth and sixth centuries, invasions and civil wars caused most existing institutions to break down. Charitable work was increasingly assumed by the emerging monastic orders. Monasteries, often established in pairs for men and women, respectively, had *infirmaries,* which were originally intended to provide care for their own *monks* and *nuns*. As the need increased, the infirmaries also began ministering to the poor and sick. Gradually the practice became formalized. The monastic orders took over the operation of most existing hospices and established many new ones throughout Europe as the Christian faith spread. The Benedictine Order, founded in the sixth century, was especially important in this movement.

In the early Middle Ages, even up to the 12th century, most monasteries did not require their members to rigidly separate themselves from the world nor to wear habits (standard dress). Within the monastery, nuns or monks chose from a variety of occupations, only one of which was nursing; in short, they were nuns or monks first, nurses second.

In addition to the monastic hospitals, some hospitals were founded by lay groups, as was the Hôtel Dieu in Lyons in 542, or by religious orders specifically devoted to nursing, as was the Hôtel Dieu in Paris, established in 650 by the Augustinian Sisters. The nursing staff directed all of these institutions, although the presiding priest had the last word on medical as well as religious matters.

Nursing at the time consisted primarily of washing the sick (less for hygiene than in imitation of Christ washing His disciples' feet); feeding the patients; making beds, (which were often vermin-ridden, since straw mattresses and other bedding were changed only three times a year—sheets were freshened somewhat more frequently); and urging the patients to pray. Nursing nuns and monks usually arose at around 5 a.m. As the patients awoke in their separate male and female wards, the nurses washed them, gave them their clothes (for it was the practice to sleep in the nude), and offered them food and drink, feeding the seriously ill. Because members of monastic orders often believed in denying themselves physical comforts while providing comforts to others, hospice patients ate at least as well as the nurses, and often better. The sick were given meat, which was forbidden for most monks and nuns except during illness. Nurses could eat only after all patients had been fed. A nurse was always to be on call, and the night nurse was especially charged to see that patients were clothed when they arose during the night to use the latrines outside.

On admission of a patient, the nurse removed the patient's clothes and itemized them, to be washed and stored with any valuables. Seriously ill people normally were assigned to single beds, if possible, but less ill patients and others who stayed in the hospice, whether pilgrim, traveler, elderly, or poor, often slept two, four or even more in a large bed. No serious attempt was made to separate people ill with contagious diseases from others.

Gradually medical knowledge again came to be accepted by the Christians, although Christ was still seen as the ultimate healer and the priest would have the last word in many hospitals for centuries yet. The little ancient learning that had survived the destruction of "pagan" materials was gathered in the monasteries, where monks and nuns studied, copied, and circulated these manuscripts. Inspired by surviving herbals, many monasteries established special gardens for medicinal herbs. Monastic nurses began to gain medical experience, in addition to being charitable custodians of the sick and poor.

Monasteries also began to establish relationships with physicians and barber-surgeons, calling them in for medical consultations, and sometimes establishing regular contracts with physicians to be on call at the hospices. The physician was purely an adviser, however, and his prescriptions might be disregarded at will by nurse, priest, or patient.

While Christian Europe was moving deeper into a dark age, and Hindu India was forgetting its Buddhist medical traditions, the Islamic world was building a golden age of medicine. Much knowledge from the ancient world had been preserved in the Near East by people who had fled persecution by Romans and Christians. There it was combined with medical learning from India. Moslem hospitals were set up on the Indian model, with nurses (usually young men or older women) joining physicians, surgeons, and *apothecaries* (*pharmacists*) as part of medical teams. Wherever Islam spread, the conquerors built extensive hospital systems. Their western center at Córdoba, Spain, was said to have over 500 hospitals and a library of over 100,000 medical manuscripts. Later, as Islam declined, so did its hospital system and the practice of nursing. But the medical knowledge the Islamic culture preserved and enhanced passed back to Europe through a variety of contacts, especially medical universities in Spain (attended by some monks) and military nursing orders that were founded in the Near East during the Crusades.

The earliest, and perhaps the most famous, of these nursing orders was the Knights of St. John, often called the Hospitalers, who built their first hospital in Jerusalem in 1050. The original intention of the Knights Hospitalers was to provide a church, monastery, and hospital for the use of pilgrims passing through Moslem territory to visit the Holy Land. But as the Crusades developed, these Knights took upon themselves not only the care of the

Hospitals set up following the military nursing models were superior to earlier hospices, but all activities—including sewing a corpse into a shroud— continued to take place in open wards. (From Le Vergier d'Honneur, *reproduced from* Medicine and the Artist [Ars Medica] *by permission of the Philadelphia Museum of Art)*

sick and wounded but also military action. They established hospitals at key points along pilgrimage and crusade routes, and often donned armor to defend them.

Originally the Knights Hospitalers were all nobles, whose families were "never" to have engaged in trade or menial work. While at first a secular order, they adopted monastic vows of poverty, chastity, and obedience, and a promise to be "the serf and the slave" of their lords, the sick. In keeping with this promise, patients were served food of their choice on silver plates, with linen provided in abundance, and were given boots and sheepskin cloaks to wear to and from the outside latrines.

Soon, however, the knights (called brothers, as monks

were) began to spend most of their time fighting. Non-noble members, called *sergeants* or *servants,* were brought in to do the actual nursing, although a knight was in charge of each ward and visited it in the morning and evening. While the Knights of St. John mostly treated male patients (sometimes Moslems and Jews, in addition to Christians), they occasionally treated women as well. A related, smaller order called the Sisters of the Order of St. John was also established. Both orders built hospitals throughout the Mediterranean and Europe, with the Knights Hospitalers' headquarters retreating from Jerusalem, to Syria, to Cyprus, to Rhodes, and finally to Malta. (In modern times, they are perhaps most widely known in a fictional connection, as the group that commissioned the bejewelled black bird in the movie *The Maltese Falcon.*) The order itself later declined, although a group called the Knights of Malta still remains, and the name of St. John has been taken by many modern ambulance and relief societies.

Two other military nursing orders were prominent. The Teutonic Knights, a German order, established its first hospital in Jerusalem in 1128 but later moved to Prussia, after the expulsion of the Crusaders from the Holy Land in the late 13th century. These knights were involved primarily in military activities, however. As early as 1280, nursing duties had been turned over to female members "because service to cattle and to sick persons" was best performed by women, they believed. The order of the Knights of St. Lazarus was founded during the same period to nurse patients with leprosy, which was widespread at the time.

These innovative military nursing orders, especially the Knights Hospitalers, set the pattern for much modern hospital practice. For the first time in Christian Europe, physicians, surgeons, and often apothecaries became part of the regular hospital staff, making formal rounds accompanied by the chief nursing brother. The Knights Hospitalers introduced the idea of weekly lectures on anatomy and medicine given by the senior physician to junior physicians and nurses, making them the first large group of professionally trained nurses in Europe. They also introduced the idea of quarantine (literally a 40-day isolation) for serious contagious diseases and for the first time in Christian hospitals required that patients obey the physician's or surgeon's advice.

As the monastic orders of the time began to adopt uniform dress for their members, so did these military nursing orders. A Knight Hospitaler, for example, would wear a red habit (later black) on which was shown the eight-pointed Maltese cross. A Teutonic Knight would wear a white tunic with a black Maltese cross outlined in gold. The dress of nursing sergeants would be less elaborate. From the monastic nursing orders, especially

Distinctive uniforms were worn by the various military nursing orders. This nurse's habit marks her as a member of the Sisters of the Order of St. John, the Knights Hospitalers. (New York Academy of Medicine)

the more military ones, stem the use of uniforms to distinguish rank among the medical staff, strict discipline within hospitals, and the probationary system for nurses' advancement. The hospitals of the Knights of St. John, and those following their model, provided some of the finest nursing available for centuries.

Most medieval hospitals only slowly adopted the Hospitalers' innovations. Much nursing care continued as before, although more often supplemented by medical advice. The 12th century saw the rise of several semi-monastic orders, made up of religiously inspired lay people who worked in the world under simple vows. Among them were groups who formed lay nursing orders. At a time when the regular monastic orders were becoming rigidly isolated from the outside world, with strict rules and binding vows, these semi-monastic orders were an attractive alternative for people who wanted to serve the sick and poor but remain out in the world.

Members of these early semi-monastic nursing orders had to be extremely dedicated and willing to sacrifice their own comfort. While monastic nurses had servants working under them, semi-monastic hospital nurses did all the drudgery themselves. The Augustinian Sisters at Paris' Hôtel Dieu, for example, had to do a large wash every six weeks and a small wash every day. In the winter this meant breaking ice and standing in the freezing river to do the job.

Since the nursing groups were more or less independent, practices varied widely; no formal training and few qualifications were required. To be accepted as a novice, applicants generally had to show only that they were freeborn, celibate, debt-free, and neither leprous nor epileptic. If accepted, they worked in the hospital for a year, learning both nursing and religious duties, after which they were subject to approval by the local chapter of the order as well as the local bishop. They then became recognized nurses, donned a religious habit, and took formal vows of poverty, obedience, and chastity. The number of nursing brothers and sisters was carefully limited by the bishops, to prevent nursing orders from developing into monasteries or convents (which they were trying to curb)—and to save money.

Nurses were expected to work extremely long hours, to observe silence, and to accept the difficulties of their life without complaint. They were severely warned against pampering themselves. Nurses were required to wear nightgowns, not for their comfort, but so they could arise at any hour of the night to aid a patient. For as long as highly motivated, relatively well-educated people were available to staff these nursing orders, they provided charitable, attentive care, if not much medical aid. Such conditions did not last, however, and in the 14th and 15th centuries several widespread social changes brought about what many have called "the dark ages of nursing."

Nursing's Dark Ages

The church, seeking to sharpen the lines between religious and secular domains, forbade monks to carry out some occupations, such as surgery and law, and required existing monastic orders to be ever more cloistered and strictly ruled. Men who, in other centuries, might have gone into nursing began to move into a wider ranger of occupations, including other medical professions that were regaining importance. Meanwhile, opportunities for women became increasingly limited, since they were barred from universities. As a result, nursing during this period came to be performed mostly by women, although groups of male nurses continued to exist.

Even more drastic changes were brought about by the Black Death, the bubonic plague that spread across Europe in the mid-14th century, killing one-third of the inhabitants in some areas. The hospital system of Europe was inadequate to deal with such widespread devastation. Servants left behind when their masters fled populated areas were often forced into service as nurses. In the panic caused by the epidemic, nurses were sometimes locked up with their patients until the crisis passed. Some nurses, however, performed voluntarily. St. Catherine of Siena, for example, was a Dominican Sister who wandered the streets at night with a lighted lamp, ministering to plague victims. A new order, the Alexian Brothers, was founded during the plague, originally to bury the dead but surviving to nurse the living. The plague caused such massive disruption that neither European society nor its medical institutions were ever the same again.

These same centuries saw the rise of Protestantism, which denounced the monastic life. All across northern Europe, monasteries and hospitals were closed and religious orders, including nursing groups, were dissolved. Even Catholic monarchs in some countries closed monasteries and added the "liberated" assets to their royal treasuries. Of the hospitals that did survive, many were destroyed during the religious wars of the 16th and 17th centuries. The loss was enormous. The hospitals that survived these centuries were far different from earlier ones. While the medical knowledge of physicians and surgeons was growing, the nursing environment was declining. Even where they survived, convents attracted and educated high-born women; nursing work in understaffed, overcrowded hospitals was no longer regarded as a proper occupation for a "lady." Monastic nurses had often been well-educated in the liberal arts, while nurses in later centuries had but spotty learning, if they were literate at all. In Protestant and Catholic countries alike, nursing became almost exclusively an occupation for uneducated, often rough women.

As Protestant countries began to establish non-religious hospitals—and they did so very slowly—they had to develop their own hospital practices. Inevitably, they took much that was of monastic origin. St. Bartholomew's Hospital, which was established in London after the city officials petitioned Henry VIII for aid for the sick, is a good example of how the secular patterns developed. In the beginning, the 100-patient hospital was staffed with a *matron* and 12 other women, all of whom slept in one large room at the hospital. The matron was head of the hospital and was charged with seeing that the staff carried out their duties: feeding and assisting the patients; making the beds; washing and mending the patients' clothes and hospital linens; and—when no other job required their attention—spinning and weaving sheets for the hospital. The matron herself made two or three tours at night to see that all was in order in the wards. The nursing staff was supposed to avoid scolding, swearing, and drunkenness; keep themselves neat and clean; and not enter the men's wards after 7 p.m. in winter and 9 p.m. in summer, except in emergency. The need for such rules indicates that the nursing staff's behavior was not above reproach. Unlike the religious nursing nuns, who did nursing work as an unpaid charitable duty, receiving only room and board, these secular nurses were paid salaries. Unfortunately, in the absence of religious motivation and convent training, secular nurses had little inducement to do more than provide minimal care and shelter for their patients.

These women were often penniless or the sole support of their families. Indeed, to save money, many hospitals used women paupers from the poorhouse as "nurses." It is no wonder that the middle and upper classes avoided such nurses until the 19th century.

Most hospitals established standard dress for their staff. Uniforms varied widely; each institution chose its own color or set of colors, and specified variations in belts, aprons, and caps to indicate staff rank. Uniforms generally changed with the fashion of the time, although there continued to be some influence from the religious nursing orders. The nurse's cap probably originated from the nun's headdress, being modified over the centuries according to changing fashions. Whatever the style, these uniforms were generally of a heavy material, often unwashable and chosen not to show dirt. Questions of

Although the quality of the nursing staff declined, many hospitals in Catholic countries remained airy and well-appointed, as here in the Hôtel Dieu in Paris in around 1500. (Bibliothèque Nationale, Paris, Ms. Ea 17 rés.)

hygiene and cleanliness did not cause a change in that pattern until the 20th century.

As Protestant hospitals expanded, so did nursing staffs. At St. Bartholomew's, for example, the staff grew to 100 and the patient population grew to over 3,500 by the end of the 18th century. Gradually pay increased and working conditions improved. While the nursing staff still lived in the hospital, they more often had single rooms instead of dormitories. The staff began to establish a hierarchy. The women in charge of wards were called *sisters,* while their more senior *watchers* were called nurses. These terms had persisted through popular usage, despite unwanted association with monasticism. Nurses were able to move up in the hierarchy by promotion. Some also developed specialties for which they received extra pay, such as for night duty or operating ward duty. Like the earlier Catholic hospitals, Protestant hospitals were initially run by the nursing staff, and only gradually established associations with surgeons, *pharmacists,* and, finally, physicians. At St. Bartholomew's, for example, surgeons were supposed to be available to dress patients' wounds at least three times a week. By the end of the 16th century, physicians had begun to write the prescriptions for each patient in a book, which is the origin of the modern hospital order book or medical chart. Medicine, however, was making rapid advances, especially from the 17th century on, while nursing was standing still—or even going backwards. In the absence of a trained, intelligent nursing staff to rely upon, physicians and surgeons began to assume control of the hospitals.

Nursing in Catholic countries also went through a period of "dark ages." Unlike the medieval monastic nurses, nuns of this period often had less access to education and therefore lacked medical knowledge. Often they were overworked as well. Twenty-four-hour tours of duty were common (in secular as well as Catholic hospitals) and even 48-hour tours were sometimes assigned. In addition, as part of an increasing restriction on nuns' freedom in the interests of modesty, nursing sisters were not allowed to care for or even look at parts of the body other than the head, feet and hands. They were, therefore, unable to keep their patients clean or free from bedsores, nor could they monitor the healing of wounds. They also were often called away from nursing for religious duties.

Such was the condition of nursing in Catholic countries before the 17th century, when Vincent de Paul, a French parish priest, introduced a new secular nursing order to supplement the religious nursing orders. St. Vincent's Sisters of Charity were young women, married or unmarried, recruited from the country to assist the religious nursing nuns. Instead of religious vows, they took short-term vows amounting to renewable, year-long contracts that always required the consent of parents or husbands. During the term of such contracts, they would receive room and board from the hospital in return for their work. St. Vincent's also revived the deaconess practice of Christians caring for patients in their homes, which cloistered nuns were not allowed to do.

While the Sisters of Charity were originally untrained,

St. Vincent often gave his early contract nurses informal talks, some of which were preserved and passed on. Most revolutionary at the time was his admonition that the sisters obey the physicians, treat them with respect, and dispense medicines according to their prescriptions. At a time when nurses had sole charge of hospitals and physicians were only advisers brought in for consultation, this was most unusual. As late as the end of the 18th century, Sister de la Croix, prioress of the Augustinian Sisters who ran the Hôtel Dieu in Paris, complained that physicians should not interfere with the patients' diets and should visit only according to the schedule established a century before. She noted:

> The constant presence of the young surgeon . . . is infinitely dangerous, especially on the women's wards. Since these young men have been admitted to the wards, the Hôtel Dieu is unrecognizable; our refuges of rest, silence, and calm now echo with loud voices, threats, and sometimes ribald remarks . . . in former times . . . a young surgeon would never have dared pass by a sister without a deferential greeting; nowadays he keeps his hat on, hums a tune, and feels pleased if he hasn't mocked or insulted her . . .

In a time when the nursing nuns still regarded the priest, not the physician, as their final authority, the secular Sisters of Charity established working relationships with their physicians and surgeons, significantly raising the level of medical care in the hospitals at which they worked. By 1660, when St. Vincent died, more than 350 Sisters of Charity worked in over 70 hospitals, mostly in France and Poland; from there the order spread widely to other Catholic areas, growing to almost 12,000.

As Europeans spread out around the world, they established hospitals in their new settlements, staffed by nurses from their native countries. In Mexico in 1520, Cortés founded America's first European-style hospital, staffed by members of a nursing brotherhood. Similar hospitals were soon founded in other major Spanish colonial towns. Hospitals came later to North America, the first being the Hôtel Dieu in Sillery, Canada, which later moved to Quebec. It was founded in 1635, but it had no trained staff until 1639 when three Augustinian Sisters of Mercy arrived to run the hospital. The earliest hospital in what is now the United States was founded in Manhattan in the 1650s by the West India Company for its sick soldiers and slaves. As Bellevue Hospital, it was later combined with the city poorhouse, becoming a penitentiary and an insane asylum as well.

Most hospitals in what is now the United States were like the worst of the European secular hospitals. Poorly built and badly maintained, they were less places for the care of the sick than for the shelter of the helpless. They were staffed by untrained, ill-paid, unmotivated nurses, who were often paupers or inmates themselves. Like Bellevue, many early American hospitals served multiple functions. Hospitals whose sole purpose was the care of the sick were not founded in the United States until the mid-18th century.

A New Day

Meanwhile in Europe, efforts were made to improve nursing practice. In the 18th century, French, English, and German physicians began to write textbooks for nurses. Most nurses, being illiterate, could not read them, but other physicians and social workers could, and they spread the idea of training for nurses. Inspired by the early Christian nurses, a lay nursing group called the deaconess order was founded in many Protestant areas of Europe, most notably in the early 19th century at Kaiserswerth, a hospital on the Rhine. Pastor Theodor Fliedner and Friederike Munster, who later became the pastor's wife, wanted to establish a Protestant nursing group similar to the Sisters of Charity. First addressing the quality of the people chosen, they recruited young women of good moral character from modest families. These *deaconesses* were then given some theoretical training in medicine and pharmacy, along with some bedside teaching in practical nursing, by the physicians attached to Kaiserswerth.

Entrants to Kaiserswerth served a probationary period of one to three years, after which they promised to serve for at least five years. No salaries were provided, only a clothing allowance, along with room and board. Only women were employed, except for a few men watchers who served night duty in the men's wards.

Kaiserswerth became famous, and women came from far away to be trained as nurses. However, as the system spread to other countries, many women began to find their work requirements excessive and living conditions repressive. They left to become salaried nurses in the "free nursing" movement that later developed in Germany.

Influenced by the Kaiserswerth experience, Elizabeth Fry, an English Quaker, established the Protestant Sisters of Charity, later called the Nursing Sisters, in 1840. They were trained primarily for private nursing in the home, an area that had been much neglected. The Anglican Church also developed groups of nursing sisters who were originally untrained but later received instruction in hospital work. In the 19th century, social reform movements began to attract well-educated women, many of whom turned to nursing, a process accelerated by women's drive to open new careers.

Into this setting came Florence Nightingale, the woman whose name is probably most associated with nursing and who had enormous influence—both positive and negative—on the modern nursing movement. Like the impulses for many previous nursing reforms, hers was religious. She felt herself called to God's service at the age of 17, deciding only later that nursing would be her field. After observing at Kaiserswerth for some weeks (where she thought the nursing rather crude) and studying briefly with the Sisters of Charity in Paris,

Nightingale returned to act as superintendent of a London nursing home. There she introduced such now-standard ideas as providing patients with a bell, so they could ring for the nurse; providing lifts to bring food to each floor, so nurses would not have to fetch trays from the kitchen; and abolishing religious requirements for admission into nursing service. She recognized the widespread need for trained nurses, and was attempting to meet it when the Crimean War began. That turned her nursing energies in a quite different direction.

The British Army had virtually no nursing available for its wounded during the early days of the war. A few surgeons were provided, but they had few medical supplies: no bandages, splints, chloroform, or other drugs; no candles or lamps by which surgeons could operate; no beds or cots; and often no food or water, because no kitchen was provided and no cups or buckets

Reports of terrible conditions in Protestant hospitals—as here in New York's Bellevue Hospital in 1860, where rats crawled over sleeping patients—built support for Florence Nightingale's reforms. (Harper's Weekly, 1860)

were available for carrying water. Such conditions were not new. What *was* new was the presence of a London *Times* reporter, William Howard Russell, who not only graphically described the intolerable conditions but also, in contrast, praised the nursing services of the Sisters of Charity who were treating the French soldiers. The public outcry was enormous, and before Britain's Secretary of War could ask Florence Nightingale to take a group of nurses to the Crimea, she had already begun to form her party. She selected 14 secular nurses and 24 others from various religious nursing orders, including 10 Roman Catholic nuns. Pay was almost double the rate paid by London hospitals at the time, plus room, board, and a uniform.

When the nursing party arrived in the Crimea, however, military officers, including medical authorities, refused to accept the nurses. They considered that the clean bedding, hot soup, and hospital clothing Nightingale demanded were "preposterous luxuries," which would only "spoil the brutes." The doctors were especially bothered by what they regarded as the intrusion of society women into their male medical province, but they could be obstructive only covertly, since Nightingale had powerful political friends. Faced with this situation, she made a controversial decision: After her group's nursing services and supplies were rejected, she gave her nurses orders not to tend any patients but to occupy themselves instead with sorting linen, arranging provisions, and other such busy work, while she waited for the doctors to accept their help.

It did not take long. Within a week, as the onset of winter brought a dramatic increase in the number of patients, the doctors called for the nurses' aid. She gave her nurses orders, however, to do nothing that was not authorized by the medical staff. The order sparked open rebellion among some of her group, who felt—probably rightly—that they knew more about diet and bed care than did the medical officers. But she prevailed.

Nightingale had, for better or for worse, set the pattern

During the 1850's Florence Nightingale almost singlehandedly transformed the nursing profession. (National Library of Medicine, Bethesda, Maryland)

for modern nursing: the doctors were the supreme authority in the hospitals, and the nurses assisted them. In practice, Nightingale ran the military hospital, having the *orderlies* as well as the nurses under her. She not only organized a kitchen, a sewage system, and a laundry, but later she also added a medical lab, a post office, a savings fund for the soldiers, rest and recreation rooms, educational classes for convalescents, and other amenities now considered standard in military hospitals. She even brought in a world-famous *chef,* Alexis Soyer, to revamp the military diet. The death rate, which had been 50 to 70 percent, fell to below 10 percent under the Nightingale regime. The degree of her success exposed the measure of the medical staff's failure—and won her their continued resentment—but it also changed the image of nursing and gained wide popular support for changes in civilian nursing as well.

Avoiding the public fanfare that had been arranged for her, Nightingale returned after almost three years in the Crimea to spend the rest of her life as a semi-invalid. While she never again appeared in public, she wielded enormous influence through her friends and through her pen. The Nightingale Fund, which consisted of contributions to honor her work, was used to start a nurses' training school in 1860 at St. Thomas' Hospital in London, over the protests of the senior surgeons. Strangely enough, although Nightingale is so much associated with nurses' training, the training itself was not revolutionary; it consisted primarily of apprenticeships plus lectures from the medical staff and sisters, with the nursing students graded on their notebooks and on written and oral examinations. Nightingale herself stressed good character over formal training. Her real break with the past was in recruiting secular nurses of good family background.

Nightingale's influence spread quickly, especially in Protestant countries with active social reform and women's equality movements. In the United States, where the Civil War broke out shortly after the Crimean War, the Union Army consulted Nightingale on how to organize military nursing; Dorothea Dix (herself a social worker, not a trained nurse) was appointed Superintendent of the United States Army Nurses. Dr. Elizabeth Blackwell, the country's first woman physician, advised her on training for nurses. Dix was immediately overwhelmed by the number of women who wanted to serve, only a few of whom had any experience. To narrow the field somewhat, she posted these requirements: "No woman under thirty years need apply to serve in the government hospitals. All nurses are required to be very plain-looking women. Their dresses must be brown or black, with no bows, no curls, no jewelry, and no hoop skirts."

As in the Crimea, although medical officers resented the presence of these women, they had no alternative but to use the nurses. In 1863 the nurses were put under their direct control rather than Dix's. Even so, wherever they could, the male doctors preferred to rely on disabled soldiers or overage men, such as the poet Walt Whitman, to serve as official or unofficial nurses. The soldiers and the general population, however, were grateful to the women. While these were not trained nurses, they were highly motivated women, often well-educated and of good family, who learned quickly.

Even before the Civil War a modest nurses' training movement had begun in North America. In 1857, Dr. Elizabeth Blackwell, a friend of Florence Nightingale, had started the New York Infirmary with an all-woman staff and had included a four-month nursing program. At first they were unable to attract "the best class of women students." But after the Civil War, better-qualified women were attracted to the new training schools founded on the Nightingale model. In these years the nurses' training movement also gained the support of the medical profession, which began to see the value of educated nurses as medicine and surgery became more sophisticated.

Even so, change was gradual. In 1870, nurses' duties still included cleaning fireplaces, wards, and stairs, laundering bandages for reuse, and washing dishes, in addition to direct care of patients. Students at early training schools were given a modest living allowance and were often sent out on private nursing duty, with their fees going to the hospitals—this was in addition to working 12-hour shifts at the hospitals, with 4 hours off once a week and time for church attendance only every other Sunday. Gradually, starting in the 1880s, ward *maids* were hired to take over some of the housekeeping duties. The early schools, modeled on Nightingale's approach, emphasized ward experience over classroom instruction. At best nurses had weekly lectures during the first year of the two-year contract they signed with the hospital. Schools slowly increased the amount of training they provided, and they added a two-month probationary period. Prospective nurses began to work less and attend more classes. Because of this, by 1900 most hospitals had stopped paying allowances and some began to charge fees for the training they offered.

Unlike English hospitals, where the superintendent of nurses had sole charge of nurses' training, in the United States nurses' training was sometimes under a physician's control. As a result, the American *nursing superintendent* never had as much power in the hospital as the British matron, especially after the physicians and lay *administrators* assumed general control of the hospital system. Almost all nurses were women. Some of them were even physicians who worked as nurses because they were better accepted as such. Less than 10 percent of the

The red cross on a white background, shown on the arm of this young nurse, became a symbol of non-partisan nursing care, as did the red crescent in Moslem countries. (Frank Leslie's, 19th century)

nursing schools accepted male students, who then ended up working mostly in insane asylums.

Another major nursing movement was developing during the same period. Swiss humanitarian Jean Henri Dunant, inspired by Florence Nightingale's example, brought together delegates from several European countries with the aim of forming relief societies to care for war casualties. In 1864 the first Geneva Convention was held, out of which grew the Red Cross. Not yet the international, neutral relief society of today, the Red Cross then involved nursing groups which were attached to each national government and which often were responsible to a national war department. English nursing continued to follow an independent line. In the United States, the Red Cross—sparked originally by Clara Barton—focused more on disaster relief than on nursing. In northern Europe, however, groups of Red Cross nursing sisters began to form, based on the Kaiserswerth model.

The Swiss also started what came to be known as the "free nursing movement." In 1854, a nurses' school was set up on what was then a revolutionary principle: that nurses had a right to independent self-support, without being bound to an institution by contract nor subject to any religious test. Such ideas proved attractive to nurses, and the free nursing movement established itself strongly in northern Europe, as nurses sought independent salaried work instead of the near bond-slavery and grueling 24-hour shifts that had been their lot.

In the same period, missionary movements carried nursing to other parts of the world, to places where nursing had not been practiced before, such as China, and to places where it had declined over the centuries, such as in India and the Islamic countries. Many missionaries had medical training, and the hospitals and nursing services they set up provided prime points of contact with the people they hoped to convert. The missionaries trained members of the local population to assist them, and the resulting nursing services were adapted to the customs of a particular area. In China, for example, nurses were initially allowed to attend only their own sex, so both male and female nurses had to be trained. In India, nursing was considered an occupation fit only for the "untouchables," the lowest caste of Hindus.

By the late 19th century, trained nurses existed all over the world, most of them influenced by Florence Nightingale's work. However, a large new group of young European nurses wanted to shape their own future. To them, Florence Nightingale might be an inspiration from the past, but she posed a bar to progress in many areas. For example, because nursing schools were under local authority, training varied widely. Younger nurses led a movement to standardize training, setting minimum requirements and state licensing. Surprisingly, Nightingale opposed the plan, since it emphasized technical skill over character. The Royal British Nurses' Association—Britain's first group of professional women—was formed in 1892 over her opposition. Similarly, in Finland, where nurses were not required to "live in," the hospital complained that nursing services suffered; with Nightingale's encouragement, the government set up a paid home for nurses not unlike the probationers' home in the Nightingale schools; this was certainly a step backward for independent nursing. On the score of uniforms, too, Nightingale was conservative, opposing the idea of washable uniforms.

While Protestant nursing was changing rapidly, Catholic nursing, which for many centuries had been far superior, was slow to improve. In France, some hospitals turned away from using nuns, instead employing anyone who would accept their low fees. The result equaled the worst in Protestant nursing. Three nurses' training schools were established in the 1870s, but nuns resisted such training and most other prospective nurses were illiterate. But as public education spread, an Anglo-French doctor, Anna Hamilton, successfully introduced the Nightingale system to France. By 1907 her program was sufficiently widespread to be put under the control of the Paris Department of Public Charities. Since the Augustinian nuns had resisted training, the Hôtel Dieu in Paris was staffed by secular nurses, for the first time in centuries. Shortly thereafter, they and other religious groups accepted training, and many nuns then reentered nursing.

In southern European countries, as was also true in Latin America, change came more slowly, partly because educated women who might have benefited most from training were barred from nursing by social custom. In Eastern Europe, trained nursing was spread primarily through schools fostered by the Red Cross, especially in the years after World War I. In Russia, for example, the Russian Red Cross was given sole charge of nurses' training and of awarding to those who successfully completed set examinations the title of "nurse." As such nursing societies spread to Moslem countries, the symbol they adopted was the Red Crescent.

The latter part of the 19th century saw widespread medical advances, along with expansion of the medical profession. In the United States, physicians and surgeons responded by establishing small private hospitals throughout the country. The number of hospitals in the United States grew from 149 in 1873 to 6,762 in 1923, with a 20-fold increase in beds to 770,000. Many of these small hospitals established "training schools." The result was a wide variation in training and a waste of trained nurses, for only students worked in hospitals. Once nurses graduated, they went into private duty nursing; often when they married, they retired. Meanwhile nursing care in hospitals improved very little, because only the *teachers* and administrators were trained nurses, the rest being overworked students.

Indeed, while many physicians recognized the medical value of trained nurses, many others feared that nurses, once trained, would not be content until they were doctors. To calm the doctors' fears, nurses adopted a generally subservient attitude. Many medical practitioners continued to feel that nurses needed no skilled training—that their work was simply an extension of traditional "women's work" into the hospital setting.

By organizing into professional groups, American nurses began to make gradual headway against such opposition. In 1893 Canadian-born Isabel Hampton, superintendent and principal of Johns Hopkins Hospital Nursing School, sparked the founding of the Society of Superintendents of Training Schools for Nurses of the United States and Canada. As in Great Britain, this nursing organization was the first professional group to be organized and controlled wholly by women. Three years later the Nurses' Associated Alumnae of the United States and Canada was formed. This later became the American Nurses Association (ANA). The first nursing journals were established in Britain and America in 1888, with the *American Journal of Nursing,* which later became the organ of the ANA, being founded in 1900.

Groups such as these began to push for standardization of training and government control of nursing. While nurses were first covered by law in 1891 in the Cape Colony (now the Union of South Africa), the first actual registration of nurses was legislated in New Zealand in 1901. In the United States, nursing organizations had to fight for such licensing state by state. The first to pass a licensing law was North Carolina in 1903, followed by New Jersey, New York, and Virginia later that year. Within 20 years, all states had established some form of registration for nurses. This registration did not imply any standardization of quality. It simply indicated that the nurse had completed a recognized course of training. Upgrading nurses' training programs was a battle on a different front. In the 1890s nurses' training programs in the United States were generally extended to three years. Most hospitals simply took advantage of the additional labor time of nurses during the extra year of nursing service. But some hospitals began to move from a 12-hour day to an 8-hour day, following the lead of the Farrand Hospital in Detroit in 1891. Hospitals also began

During the decades when United States hospitals were training—but not hiring—nurses, most graduate nurses worked in private duty, treating patients at home. (Famous Paintings of the World, 1895)

to establish six-month preparatory training courses for nursing students before they were given any ward duties.

Medical men had some grounds for concern about competition from nurses in the United States; nurses' training in that period was in many ways superiors to their own. While, before the turn of the century, neither doctors nor nurses needed high school diplomas in order to enter training, the training program for nurses was generally three years long, while that for physicians and dentists was often shorter, sometimes as short as one year. And because nurses' training programs had developed from apprenticeship programs (remaining very much in that tradition in Europe), nursing schools had used clinical demonstrations since the early 1890s; physicians, however, were still receiving their education mostly from books.

Modern Nurses

On the eve of the Depression, nurses' training was still variable, and the oversupply of trained private-duty nurses and undersupply of trained hospital nurses had grown acute. As a result, a national committee on nursing schools recommended the closing of most small (under 50 beds), unaccredited hospital schools; the committee also suggested closing schools that did not include at least four registered nurses on the hospital staff or that used students to act as head nurses or supervisors. In the desperate economic conditions that followed the 1929 stock market crash many small hospitals did close their schools, if only because graduate nurses were sometimes willing to work in hospitals for just room and board. The number of hospital schools dropped by one-third in just a decade. Many other unemployed nurses were put to work in government programs during the 1930s and, as the hospital system grew, registered nurses increasingly made up hospital staffs. While, in 1927, almost three-quarters of all United States hospitals employed no graduate nurses, that was true of only 10 percent of the hospitals a decade later. The change was not welcomed by all nurses, since many hospitals still required that nurses live on the hospital grounds, or that they work a "split shift" which extended over 12 hours, even though they worked only eight—for example, four hours on duty, four hours off, and another four hours on.

World War II drew a major demarcation line in modern nursing. In many countries, nurses were given full military rank for the first time. Oddly enough, rank was accorded only to women, since nursing was strongly considered a female profession; male nurses during the war were ranked only as enlisted men. Separate nursing units were formed within the various armed services, and nurses served in combat areas around the world—often wearing fatigues instead of the white uniforms that had come to be common in the interwar period. Nurses gained

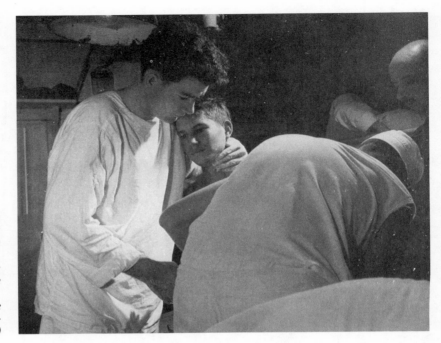

Male nurses and orderlies formed an important part of the medical teams ministering to the wounded in World War II, like this young private being tended on a hospital ship in the Pacific Ocean in April 1945. (From General Records of the Department of the Navy, 1798-1947, #80-G-413963)

a status and independence through this war service, and the new prestige carried over into civilian life after the war.

Postwar developments such as national health insurance plans put hospitals at the center of the health-care system. Increasing medical sophistication meant that, as doctors specialized, nurses took over functions previously closed to them, such as giving intravenous injections. Expansion of duties led to the development of different levels of nursing. As registered nurses took on increasingly skilled functions in many countries, *practical nurses,* who were given short training courses, assumed some less skilled nursing functions. In certain areas, they were given separate licensing as a Licensed Practical Nurse (LPN) or Licensed Vocational Nurse (LVN). *Nurses' aides* were employed to carry out the many non-nursing duties involved in running hospitals, functions that previously had been performed by nursing students. In some countries, no distinction was made between practical nurses and nurses' aides, with the less trained nursing staff simply being called *auxiliaries*.

As college education grew more widespread, colleges assumed the job of training nurses; those nurses who wanted to enter teaching or administration often had to gain a bachelor's degree or even complete postgraduate work in addition to nursing programs. In most American and European countries such nursing programs are still ends in themselves, with graduates tending to remain nurses. Some other countries, however, follow the model developed by the Soviet Union. There, the whole medical profession represents a single career ladder up which people can move: those with general education and a little practical training are aides or orderlies; those with eight to ten years of general education and an additional three to four years of training are nurses, midwives, or lower-level physicians; those with even more general education and medical training can qualify as physicians.

Social changes after the war began to transform nursing in other ways. United States hospitals historically had been separated by color. Because almost all nursing schools refused to accept black students, separate schools were set up, the first being at Provident Hospital in Chicago in 1891, then at Howard University (later Freedman's Hospital) in Washington, D.C., in 1893. The national American Nurses Association did not draw a color line and indeed carried individual black nurses on their rolls, but many state chapters barred black members. A separate National Association of Colored Graduate Nurses was formed in 1908. During World War II, the nursing services—like the fighting forces—were segregated. Not until the late 1940s did the military nursing corps become integrated, and only then did the United States government begin to pressure nursing schools and hospitals to integrate.

After World War II, men also began to enter nursing in larger numbers. The proportion of male nurses, small at the turn of the century, had continually declined over the decades; in the United States, only 2 percent of all nurses were male in 1940. Victims of reverse bias, they were discriminated against by the nursing schools, by the wording of organization bylaws, and by government statutes. In addition, they had to contend with job titles that were universally regarded as feminine, such as "sister" or "matron" in Great Britain. However, the years since World War II have seen increasing status for nurses, higher standards of education, better pay and working conditions, and a wide variety of job opportunities, all of which have led to an increase in the number of male nurses in many parts of the world.

The 20th century has also seen the development of a number of nursing specialties, some of recent vintage and some reaching back far into history. One of the oldest nursing specialties is that of *psychiatric nurse*. The mentally ill were traditionally regarded as either criminals or people possessed by demons, rather than as potential recipients of nursing care. Probably the first organized care for mentally ill and retarded people was centered in Gheel, Belgium, in the early Middle Ages.

Gheel was a special case, however. During medieval times, the only nursing order that accepted insane patients was the Hospitalers of St. John. When they left Jerusalem, their hospital was continued as an asylum for the insane by the Moslems. Not until the 14th century was another mental hospital established, Bethlehem Hospital in London, more commonly known as "Bedlam." But Bedlam and other such hospitals were for many centuries more like prisons than hospitals. The nurses acted as jailers who presided over chained patients, administering early forms of "shock therapy," such as dunking patients in ice water or whirling them around upside down strapped in chairs. Given this view of "treatment," it is not surprising that most male nurses, stronger and thought to be better able to subdue patients, worked in psychiatric hospitals. It was not until after World War II that psychiatric nursing began to shift from custodial care to positive therapy.

Nurses have also developed specialties within hospital service. Some have become highly trained *surgical nurses*. In the pre-anesthetic centuries, when surgeons relied on speed and strength, attending nurses had little to do but restrain the patient and hold a pan to catch the blood. Once anesthetics gave surgeons time to apply newly developed techniques and skills, they required trained nursing assistants, people who worked regularly as part of an operating team. Indeed, the rubber gloves that are now a standard part of the operating room costume were developed when a "scrub nurse," Caroline Hampton, developed a skin allergy to the antiseptic solutions introduced around 1880. Her fiancé, a surgeon, had rubber gloves made for her and, when the rest of the operating team adopted them, infection dropped to near zero. Another specialty is the *nurse anesthetist*. Interns were initially used to administer anesthetics, but nurses began to do so in the Mayo Clinic in Rochester, Minnesota, in 1889. The practice spread and a special course for nurse anesthetists was established in Portland, Oregon, in 1909. Some questions were raised about whether, in administering anesthetics, nurses were practicing medicine. Legal opinion has since indicated that such actions are proper, if performed under the direction of a physician or dentist. With the complexity of modern surgery, however, most such administration today is handled by specialist physicians called *anesthesiologists,* except in very rural areas or undeveloped countries.

As medical practice grew more sophisticated, the focus of nursing care shifted. After World War II, hospitals became centers of medical care for the whole population, not just the poor and homeless. Health insurance helped absorb some of the increased medical costs. Certain countries, like those in northern Europe, established national health services to help ensure that medical aid reached every citizen. However, the disparity in the quality of medical care between city and country, between affluent neighborhoods and rundown slums and, perhaps most of all, between developed and un-

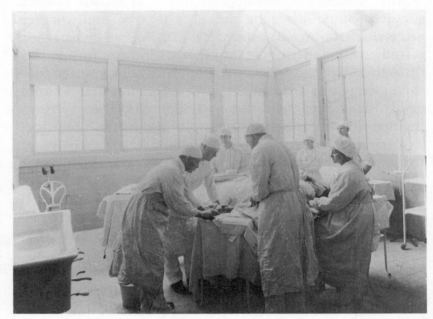

In early 20th-century operations, anesthetics were often dripped from a sponge onto a gauze mask covering the patient's face, a job being performed by the nurse-anesthetist on the right. (National Library of Medicine, Bethesda, Maryland)

developed countries continued to grow. For example, in parts of the United States one nurse is available for every 230 people, while in parts of Africa the ratio is more like one to 12,500. *Public health nursing* emerged as a major specialty dedicated to redressing that balance.

Modern public health nursing came out of the widespread movement for social reform in the 19th century, and—like so many other changes in nursing—was sparked by Florence Nightingale. Called on by a Liverpool philanthropist, William Rathbone, to help solve the medical problems of the poor, she advised him on setting up a visiting or district nurse program (much like the original deaconesses of Roman times). Later she helped him set up a school to provide trained nurses. The visiting nurse movement spread from there, developing along with social work, at first as part of private philanthropy, later under government supervision. Traditionally, public health nurses have worked in the poorest areas, including those where recent immigrants and refugees have settled, or in rural or "bush" areas like the Outback in Australia or parts of the American Appalachians. In recent decades the World Health Organization (WHO) has sent many nurses to countries around the world, to provide primary nursing care and also to teach nursing to the local population, particularly in those countries where medical care had previously been provided by colonial or missionary nurses.

The increasing responsibility taken on by nurses in such programs, where doctors are scarce or nonexistent, and the expanding range of medical techniques has led to the formation of a new specialty, intermediate between that of the registered nurse and the physician or surgeon. The title for this specialty varies, including *nurse practitioner, physician's assistant, surgeon's assistant,* or (in the Soviet Union) *feldsher.* Whatever the name, these specialists are (following additional training) allowed to perform functions previously done only by physicians, such as taking patient histories, running pediatric clinics, or "harvesting" veins from a patient's leg, to be used in a cardiac bypass operation.

Another specialty that developed out of the public health nursing movement was that of *nurse-midwife.* These are registered nurses who have received advanced training in obstetrics and in infant and maternal care. They generally operate at the level of the nurse practitioner. Nurse-midwives have been especially active in northern Europe, attending at many normal births and calling in obstetricians only if difficulties are encountered. However, in the United States, nurse-midwives have faced the opposition of physicians (who have tried to keep childbirth completely in the hands of obstetricians) and have been allowed to operate only where doctors are scarce or unwilling to serve. Even then, many nurse-midwives have either been European or have trained in Europe. In recent decades the nurse-midwife movement has revived somewhat in the United States, and it has spread even further throughout Europe.

Up to about 1910, nurses and aides were the only two

kinds of health-care workers assisting physicians and surgeons. As hospital-centered health care became more technical and sophisticated, however, a whole new range of medical occupations came into existence in the highly industrialized countries. At first called *paramedical workers,* the term *allied health workers* has become more common in the United States, while in other developed countries they are called *ancillary* or *auxiliary medical workers.* Estimates of the number of new allied health specialties developed by the 1970s range from 450 to 600, although that includes many jobs with overlapping functions or the same functions with different names.

Originally many such occupations were entry-level jobs, requiring no experience, special training, or high school diploma. The earliest technicians and technologists in hospitals were generally aides who learned special skills through on-the-job training and later in-service lectures. *X-ray technicians* and *electrocardiograph/electroencephalograph technicians* are two specialties that emerged as new technology was introduced and people were trained on the job to use the new equipment. As clinical testing, analysis, and diagnosis became a more important part of medical care, a whole range of *medical laboratory technologists* and *technicians* came to be developed. Aides increasingly took over non-nursing functions from nurses, and some record-keeping activities were delegated to *medical record technicians* or *clerks.* Other traditional jobs expanded as more sophisticated approaches were developed. Aides who once carried patients on stretchers to hospitals later became *ambulance drivers* (often volunteers). Today in many places these aides have become *emergency medical technicians* (EMT), trained in such modern emergency techniques as cardiopulmonary resuscitation (CPR). When in radio consultation with doctors, they sometimes administer drugs and use artificial resuscitation equipment.

Some national and state governments have begun to require licensing of various allied health occupations, a trend somewhat hindered by differing definitions and overlapping functions of various specialties. As the specialties become defined, however, the tendency has been for special training courses to be developed in technical or vocational institutes or community colleges. In practice, many allied health workers on hospital night shifts carry out activities that, during the day, would be carried out only by physicians, surgeons, or registered nurses.

Like nurses, allied health workers have traditionally been predominately female but, as technological and technical jobs have proliferated, men have moved into the area. One of the fastest growing occupational groups in heavily settled industrialized countries, allied health workers still have relative low status and high turnover. This is because of the lack of licensing and job definition, which leads to uncertain advancement or to dead-end jobs, and because of the traditional hard work, difficult hours, and understaffing in many hospitals, especially those in the inner cities.

Some other health-related occupations have more independent histories and require higher education and specialized training. Diet and nutrition have played an important part in medical care at least since early Egypt. While physicians counseled on diet as part of their medical advice, for many centuries hospital diets were under the control of the nursing staff. As non-nursing functions were delegated to aides, and as physicians gradually assumed control of the hospitals in the last century or so, the specialty of the *dietitian* emerged. This person is responsible for planning and supervising healthful meals. Dietitians today work in hospitals and nursing homes, as well as in schools and other large institutions, where they plan and supervise food preparation and service. Others work in research and education, while some, often called *nutritionists,* work in community health programs.

Physical therapy also has a long history. Hydrotherapy massages have been prescribed by medical advisers in almost all cultures. The Egyptians, Greeks, and Chinese used hot mineral baths. American Indians and Scandinavians had sweat huts, the use of which was sometimes followed by immersion in cold water or snow. The Chinese buried patients up to their necks in hot sand packs. *Masseurs* have also been widely used, with blind masseurs often being preferred for reasons of privacy and modesty. Levers and pulleys to stretch or straighten the body have been used at least since Alexandrian times. The Italian physician Luigi Galvani pioneered in electrophysiology in the late 18th century. These and some other techniques have existed for thousands of years, but the profession of *physical therapist* has arisen only in the 20th century. Two world wars, modern poliomyelitis epidemics, and industrial accidents produced many people, often quite young, in need of relief and rehabilitation, at a time when the popular conscience was being raised by social reformers.

The earliest physical therapists were associated with military hospitals, and many modern physical therapy techniques originated in such settings. But increasingly physical therapy has been associated with public hospitals, especially as outpatient hospital services have expanded since World War I. A physical therapist must have at least a bachelor's degree, although some master and doctoral programs exist. Therapists are licensed in all parts of the United States and in most other industrialized countries. They work under the direction of physicians, surgeons, dentists, and especially *orthopedic surgeons* or specialists in physical medicine, sometimes called *physiatrists,* who are medical doctors focusing on these areas of care.

Other forms of therapy have split off to become separate specialties in some industrialized countries. *Respiration therapists,* sometimes called *inhalation therapists,* use modern techniques and machinery to restore and maintain breathing in emergency and other longer-term medical situations. *Speech pathologists* and *audiologists* work to help people overcome speaking and hearing disabilities. *Occupational therapists* help people achieve or regain skills they need for self-sufficiency, while *art therapists, music therapists,* and *recreation therapists* help people develop or revive those skills that can help them enjoy normal lives.

Allied health specialties are commonly confined to the metropolitan areas of industrialized countries. They are rare in rural and poor areas, especially in developing countries, where medical personnel generally perform a wide range of functions. Such specialties are likely to increase as better medical care becomes more widely available in such areas, just as the number of allied health workers in the United States jumped from less than 250,000 to over two million in the first 70 years of the 20th century. But the shortage of skilled health-care personnel may well continue. Recruitment is often insufficient to meet the need and, in the developed countries, nursing must now compete for the best candidates with many other professions, including the higher-status medical occupations. Even within the profession, many nurses choose to work in other settings, such as schools, industries, insurance companies, and private clinics, rather than in the more demanding hospital system.

Nursing was built, over the centuries, on sacrifice and duty. This often translated into exploitation of nurses who were motivated by charitable impulses and, sometimes, into exploitation of patients by unprincipled nurses, especially in later centuries. At times seen as little more than an extension of "women's work," nursing has developed from simple custodial care to include a whole range of specialties, some of them demanding highly skilled personnel and all of them vital in modern society.

For related occupations in this volume, *Healers,* see the following:
Midwives and Obstetricians
Pharmacists

Physicians and Surgeons
Psychologists and Psychiatrists

For related occupations in other volumes of the series, see the following:

in *Helpers and Aides:*
Bath Workers
Child Nurses
Servants and Other Domestic Laborers
Social Workers
Undertakers

in *Restaurateurs and Innkeepers:*
Prostitutes

in *Scholars and Priests:*
Priests
Monks and Nuns
Teachers

in *Warriors and Adventurers:*
Soldiers

Pharmacists

Pharmacy developed out of early medicine at a time when it was intertwined with religion. Initially, the *priest-physicians* themselves prepared medicines, the earliest known medical prescription being written down in Sumer over 2000 years B.C. During the same period, in the temples that were Egypt's medical centers, priest-physicians began to employ assistants to prepare medicines, either mixing them on demand or preparing them for future use. These early *pharmacists* pioneered in setting measurements of drugs in prescriptions, testing drug doses on slaves and prisoners, who were considered expendable. The standard volume and weight measures established by the Egyptians are very close to those still in use today. People were also delegated to collect drugs, not only herbs grown locally but also animal parts and

Like this Roman woman shown preparing medicines with an assistant, some women have always engaged in pharmacy, either as apothecaries or as sages femmes, or wise women. (Musée des Antiquités Nationales, St.-Germain-en-Laye)

excrement, which were used in medicines. The Egyptians sent raiding parties into Africa for some medicinal items and imported drugs and spices from as far away as India and China, all to be stored in royal warehouses until needed. These collectors and *importers* were the earliest practitioners of the importing side of pharmacy, which was and still is both a profession and a trade.

In the same period, the early Indian and Chinese civilizations were developing medical works that focused on herbs. In China, the earliest *materia medica,* or study of the preparation and uses of remedies, was written around 2700 B.C., supposedly by the Chinese emperor Shen Nung, who was said to have collected all the herbs listed himself. Chinese diseases were classified as either hot or cold, and drugs were classified likewise; heating drugs were to be gathered in daylight during hot weather and prepared by heating or boiling, while cooling drugs were to be gathered at night in cold weather and prepared by soaking in cool water. Medicines were prepared not only as liquids, but also as pills and powders. Herbs were imported in India as well, where their medicinal properties were enhanced by the belief that plants were friendly to humans. In the vast chain of hospitals that were erected later in Buddhist India, each had an herbal garden attached.

In south and east Asia, drugs were considered so important a part of medical treatment that no mere specialist was allowed to prepare them. In India, the physician was charged with personally selecting, gathering, and preparing the herbal medicine to be used, although an apprentice might assist in the process. Special chants were designed to ensure that the herb's strength remained in the medicine. The Chinese went even further. Throughout much of their history, highborn Chinese would not even allow physicians to prepare medicines for them; instead a family's eldest son (whose general education included some medical training for this purpose) was supposed to prepare medicine according to a physician's prescription, test it on himself, and only then give it to the patient. Even poorer people often prepared their own medicines. In China they sometimes followed prescriptions that were posted at crossroads to assist them. To serve these people of south and east Asia, there developed a group of *apothecaries,* small *shopkeepers,* who collected, prepared, sold, and traded herbs in their own areas as well as with other countries, such as Egypt.

For a long time specialists in pharmaceutical preparation existed only in the Near East. They were often merely assistants to physicians, who (as in the Far East) usually prepared their own medicines. That pattern was adopted in early Greece where Asclepius, the god of healing, was said to be assisted by the goddess Hygieia, who compounded his remedies. Hygieia was pictured with a healing serpent twined around one arm and a bowl in the other, the two becoming a modern symbol of pharmacy. The double-edged effect of many medicines is reflected in the Greek word *pharmakon,* which meant "remedy" but also carried the meaning of "poison." Greek physicians were assisted by a group of *rhizotomoi* (root-cutters), who found and gathered herbs for them. In addition, a group of street *druggists* sold love potions and other such remedies directly to the public.

In later Greece and in Rome, to which Greek medicine spread, physicians increasingly relied on specialists to prepare drugs. Unfortunately, more typical of late Roman pharmaceutical preparations was *theriac.* According to Galen, Mithridates, king of Pontus in the first century B.C., experimented on criminals with mineral and vegetable poisons and antidotes. He later mixed together all the antidotes he knew, to provide a universal remedy he called *mithridatium.* In the next century, Andromachus, physician to Nero's court, revived this "universal antidote," calling it theriac. Since theriac could include anything the apothecary wished to get rid of, its popularity was a license for abuse. (Later known as "treacle," this type of mixture continued to be sold by apothecaries until the 19th century.)

When Christianity rose to dominance in the fourth century A.D., medical centers came to be regarded as pagan and most were closed. Only two centuries later, the Western Roman Empire itself collapsed and, with it, most remaining medical structures. Much general medical learning, including pharmaceutical knowledge, was lost to the West. Apothecaries did, however, continue to import and prepare medications, passing their knowledge on through the apprenticeship system. Even where physicians remained, especially in the Byzantine Empire, apothecaries ministered directly to the poorer classes, in addition to preparing drugs for physicians. They also supplied herbs to the local *midwives* or *sages femmes* (wise women), who likewise dispensed medical treatment to the poor, as well as providing herbs to women treating their own families, which was common practice in the Middle Ages. In many cases, these apothecaries were little more than *greengrocers,* with whom they later formed guilds in some areas.

In south and east Asia, apothecaries also continued to be essentially specialist greengrocers. But, unlike in Western countries, the cultivation of medicinal herbs was considered to be so important that, in some places, the whole process was organized under government supervision. In sixth-century-A.D. China, herb farms were established throughout the country, under the direction of the medical bureau. Young men in their late teens were brought in as apprentices, learning when to plant, how to cultivate, when to harvest, and how to store properly all the main herbs in the Chinese *materia medica.* Although people generally continued to prepare their own medicines, apothecary shops became fixtures in Chinese cities. Druggists formed guilds and worshipped the legendary herbal physician Shen Nung as their patron god, making offerings at his shrine and giving a 10 percent discount in his honor on certain days. In later centuries, especially between the 11th and 14th centuries, public pharmacies were established by the government as part of a welfare policy for the poor.

Meanwhile, the Islamic golden age of medicine emerged. Much of the medical learning of Egypt, Greece, and Rome had survived in the Near East, preserved by Christian and Jewish refugees from the Roman world. Knowledge from further east arrived there, too, especially from nearby India. In the Moslem Near East there developed for the first time a clearly independent class of pharmacists, who were not simply greengrocers or physicians' assistants. Many historians date the first modern pharmacies from the opening of apothecary shops in the bazaars of early ninth-century Baghdad. Pharmacists in the main Islamic cities at this time were trained, examined, and licensed. Whether they prepared medicines primarily for physicians or directly for patients, whether they worked in privately owned shops or in hospital laboratories or dispensaries, their work was routinely checked by inspectors. Prepared medicines were shipped by caravans from major cities throughout the Islamic world and beyond. The hospital at Damascus, for example, prepared medicines for the surrounding area, including distilled alcohol used for medical purposes. A Jewish visitor in the late Middle Ages wrote that the fires in the laboratories of the Damascus Hospital had never gone out since they were lit shortly after the hospital was built in 1160.

Among the pharmacists working in these laboratories were *alchemists*. These early scientists sought the secret of making gold and silver out of cheaper, "baser" metals. Because what they sought was not scientifically possible and involved them in a great deal of mysticism, alchemists and the study of alchemy in later times became discredited. But, in fact, alchemists developed many of the laboratory techniques basic to pharmacy and chemistry, sciences that later took the place of alchemy. Alchemists working in the Moslem pharmacies generally sought to discover and refine new medicines, as in modern pharmacology, rather than simply preparing large amounts of standard medicines, as in traditional pharmacy. In addition to these pharmacists, an unregulated group of apothecaries continued to operate as small shopkeepers, selling spices, cosmetics, and some medicines.

As contacts between Christian and Islamic cultures increased, medical learning, including pharmaceutical knowledge, filtered back into Europe. The Christian church gradually relaxed its outright ban on "pagan" medicine, and herb gardens became fixtures in monasteries and convents. The apothecary Damian, a

Christian martyred in the early fourth century (along with his physician-brother, Cosmas), was celebrated as the patron saint of pharmacy. As medicine was admitted into monasteries, monks and nuns began to specialize in the preparation of medicines, copying and studying the few pharmacopeia (encyclopedias of drug information), like that of the Greek herbalist Dioscorides, which had survived in Europe. These were supplemented by medical writings from the Islamic world. In Europe's new medical schools, the first in Salerno in the ninth century, *materia medica* courses were made part of the curriculum for physicians. International trade in medicines also received official attention. In Venice, for example, the drug trade was under government supervision from the 12th century on.

Like many early pharmacists, this German apothecary is preparing medicines in his open-sided street shop. The cone-shaped items on the shelves are sugar, sold along with spices and candies by apothecaries in this era. (By Jost Amman, from The Book of Trades, *late 16th century)*

However, the Islamic model of trained, state-regulated pharmacists was not followed in Europe for some centuries. The first attempt to regulate pharmacists in Christian Europe was made in the Kingdom of the Two Sicilies by Frederick II, the Holy Roman Emperor, in the 1230s. He decreed that apothecaries and physicians should practice independently, with physicians not allowed to be either owners or partners in apothecary shops. Apothecaries had to prepare drugs according to the prescribed method and at a price specified by law. In addition, inspectors were appointed to assure that the apothecary's work was reliable, produced according to the physician's prescription, and at the proper price. Failure to obey the law was punishable by seizure of drugs and even, in extreme cases, by death. The government also limited the number of pharmacies allowed in a given area. While not all of these regulations were uniformly adopted in Europe—nor have they been so even today—they formed the pattern toward which government regulation in most of mainland Europe tended.

The aim of Frederick II's law was to separate the healing profession from the profit-making trade in drugs. However, it left open the question of who could dispense medical advice. Apothecaries therefore continued to do so, giving grounds for battle between apothecaries and physicians, a battle which lasted into the 20th century in many parts of the world. Paris officials in the 14th century began to define more clearly the relationship between apothecary and physician. Before being allowed to practice, the apothecary had to swear:

> . . . to do nothing rashly without the advice of Physicians and only in the hope of gain. To give no medication or purge to those laboring under any disease, without first taking counsel of some learned doctor. . . . To dispense exactly, without adding or leaving out anything in the prescriptions of the doctors, as far as they are in accordance with the rules of the art.

In the 15th century, some German cities began establishing apothecary shops at state expense, with ordinary medicines provided free to the public. The apothecary was given, variously, a salary, an annual supply of food and drink, and/or an exemption from obligations to the local parish. Among these public apothecaries were women as well as men, reflecting the fact that *sages femmes* had locally dispensed medical advice for many centuries. Women often learned the apothecary's trade working with their fathers or husbands, sometimes taking over the business on their own. In this same period, governments in France, Germany, and Italy began to restrict the sale of poisons; some required a permit from a physician or surgeon stating the purpose for which the poison would be used, and others forbade sale to *slaves, servants,* minors or strangers.

In this same period, pharmacists, like other people in trades and professions, began to form guilds. These regulated production and distribution, served social and welfare functions, and set standards for the trade. In the major cities of Italy, France, and Germany, physicians and pharmacists tended to be members of the same guild. One of the earliest such guilds was formed in Florence in the late 1100s. In 1236, when the city's trade guilds were divided into two classes, the physicians and pharmacists guild was classed with the "major arts." These Italian guilds were unusual in being important political organizations, but throughout continental Europe, pharmacists had very high status, equivalent to that of physicians. Most guilds focused on internal regulation of their trade, including supervision of admission, education, examination, and limitation of the number of pharmacies. In a few cases, especially in Germany, state or local authorities exercised some of this control. Where the number of pharmacies was limited, the privilege of owning a pharmacy was extremely valuable. In some areas, like Germany, pharmaceutical "dynasties" emerged where the same family operated a pharmacy for many generations.

In more rural parts of Europe, especially in England, where too few apothecaries existed to form a guild, they were lumped into a guild with many other retailers. Such an association, emphasizing the trade aspects of the apothecary's profession, carried less status than on the Continent. Greengrocers, *spicers, pepperers,* and other such dealers in herbs and vegetables were the apothecary's natural competitors. In rural areas apothecaries might be awarded a monopoly in all such retail goods in order to provide them with enough income for their support. Since university-trained physicians were rare and generally lived only in the cities, apothecaries often operated as the main medical advisers

The supposed universal antidote theriac, *later called* treacle, *continued to be made in the Middle Ages, sometimes under municipal supervision following a set formula, but more often as a chemical stew made from an apothecary's leftover drugs. (From* Das Neu Distiller Buch, *National Library of Medicine, Bethesda, Maryland)*

to country or poor people. Some even combined pharmaceutical work with surgery (both apprenticeship occupations), acting in essence as general practitioners.

In the 1500s, the practice of pharmacy began to change with the discovery of the Americas, where—to the Europeans' surprise—they found a sophisticated medical system. When Cortés arrived in Tenóchtitlan, capital of the Aztec Empire, in 1519, he reported: "Houses were found in which they kept pharmacies where remedies ready to drink, ointments, and plasters can be bought." Explorers also reported to Spain that no doctors need be sent to Peru, since Inca physicians had more effective cures. Indeed, the Incas had people appointed to collect herbs and to guard the coca plantations. Traveling apothecaries would tour around the countryside with their stock of medicines. The arrival of new drugs from the Americas, including tobacco, ipecac, and curare, demonstrated that the medieval pharmacopeias, based on Classical and Islamic books, were not the final word. This outlook in turn spurred experimentation and research in new medicines.

One of the main figures in the deliberate search for new medicines was the Swiss physician Philippus II Paracelsus, who stressed the use of chemicals, rather than herbs alone, as medicines. Early alchemists, while following a wrong track scientifically, had developed chemical laboratory techniques such as distillation and extraction. As Paracelsus put it: "It is not the task of alchemy to make gold, to make silver, but to prepare medicines." He laid the basis for modern pharmacology, establishing its close relationship to modern chemistry, which emerged along with it.

During this period, pharmacies began to move into larger-scale production of medicines, especially when they were located near the sources of rare raw materials and in port cities from which materials might easily be shipped. The hand-grinding of medicines with mortars and pestles gave way in some firms to grinding by horse-powered mills. Some of the family pharmacies that had existed for generations expanded into pharmaceutical firms, a few of which still exist today. The international Merck organization, for example, grew from a 17th-century family pharmacy in Darmstadt, Germany. Large-scale production created the demand for storage containers; pharmacies therefore played a major role in the development of the modern pottery industries. At some times and places, certain container shapes were even restricted for pharmaceutical use. The elegant drug jars not only served functional purposes, but also gave pharmacies the artistic look that apothecaries thought suitable to their status in society.

Despite attempts to keep separate the functions of physician and apothecary, the two often worked closely together. Physicians sometimes examined patients in the apothecary shop, or had patients referred to them by the apothecary. Sometimes the relationship was so valuable that, where it was allowed, a physician would also obtain a pharmacist's license. With their high social status, many apothecaries assumed responsibilities other than mere preparation of medicines. Apothecaries often held important political positions, especially in Italy; in France and Germany, apothecaries were given military rank equal with that of physicians, and they were often given substantial administrative duties.

As apothecaries began to focus more on the high-status aspects of their profession, others began to move into the trade of pharmacy. Gradually there developed a class of *drogisten* or (*druggists*) who specialized in selling all those materials that were not specifically restricted to pharmacies, such as cosmetics, diet aids, spices, and dyes.

Far less reputable, but ever-present in this period, as in others, were rank charlatans who sold worthless remedies from back packs on the street and sometimes gave medicine shows to catch the public's attention. While some remedies were harmless, consisting mostly of sugar, others were ineffective and potentially dangerous. Most notable was the craze for "mummy-

The carved furniture, open space, and absence of pharmaceutical equipment all indicate the high status of this 16th-century German apothecary, here shown with a physician selecting drugs from distinctively marked pottery containers. (Reproduced from Medicine and the Artist [Ars Medica] *by permission of the Philadelphia Museum of Art)*

powder" as a medicine, a craze that lasted until the 18th century in some places. Some of this substance was apparently derived from actual mummies imported from Egypt and ground up for the purpose, but much of it was from "instant mummies," bodies from paupers' graves wrapped in linen and burned, the ashes sold to a gullible public.

A change in medical fashion further transformed pharmacies in this period. From the 14th through 18th centuries in continental Europe enemas, called clysters, were extremely popular. Clysters were administered by apothecaries who used large syringes filled with medicated fluid. When the clyster fad finally began to pass, apothecaries became choice targets for artistic wits, including Molière and Daumier. Such ridicule was so successful that it may have spurred apothecaries to adopt a new name.

From the 17th century on European apothecaries began to call themselves *pharmacien,* (*pharmacists*). These continental pharmacists, with their change of name, maintained the high social standing of apothecaries. Indeed, their scientific activities continued the growth of their profession. Many of the innovators who founded modern chemistry were originally pharmacists. Even today in parts of Europe, especially France and Germany, pharmacists perform or supervise much of the medical laboratory work required by physicians.

The apothecary's occupation developed very differently in the British Isles. England did not have the tradition of pharmaceutical regulation that existed on the Continent. It also had a chronic shortage of trained physicians, especially in the rural areas. As a result, apothecaries routinely dispensed medical advice along with remedies, especially in poor or rural areas. As on the Continent, many apothecaries also doubled as surgeons. Physicians complained and brought legal suits against apothecaries, but were hampered in their suits by public opinion. Apothecaries clearly served a social need that would go unmet if the giving of medical advice was restricted to physicians. Also, during the plague epidemics of the 1600s, apothecaries generally continued to serve the sick, while many physicians fled.

As British apothecaries increasingly focused on medical activities, the pharmaceutical field was sometimes left unfilled. Many physicians began to prepare their own medications due to the shortage of apothecaries, who had become their medical colleagues and competitors.

However, as in continental Europe, other groups soon moved into the drug trade to fill the gap. In the British Isles the two main groups, with overlapping functions, came to be druggists, who were primarily grocers or wholesalers, and *chemists,* who were skilled in laboratory work and could prepare a wide variety of chemical substances.

In the United States, the situation was even further complicated. In the absence not only of government regulation but also of guild controls, pharmacy developed in an entirely haphazard way. Colonial settlers brought with them the medical patterns of their native countries, and the frontier soon blurred European distinctions. Anyone with a little medical knowledge would be called upon to provide a very wide range of services. An apothecary might easily act as physician, surgeon, *dentist,* and *veterinarian.* Similarly, many a grocer took on the role of an apothecary, simply by virtue of carrying a supply of herbs and medicaments. In the days before government control the public made little distinction between a physician's dispensary, an apothecary shop, and a general store. Indeed, on the frontier, the public often had no choice; they had to take what was available. In such circumstances, the popularity of so-called patent medicines—cheap remedies that promised to be cure-alls—is easy to understand.

The tangled relationships between apothecaries and their competitors, the physicians and grocers, did not really sort themselves out until the 19th century, with the introduction of formal training for pharmacists. In Europe, the traditional training for an apothecary had, for many centuries, consisted of two to five years of apprenticeship (which involved learning Latin) plus four to ten years of work as an apothecary's assistant before one was eligible to apply for an apothecary's privilege. Local and, later, national guilds supervised and examined potential applicants, with governments and physicians also sometimes having a hand in the process. In the mid-16th century, France began to require

Apothecaries were often handy targets for wit, as in this turn-of-the-19th-century drawing of an English apothecary treating the blistered seat of a discommoded rider. The sign indicates that he doubles as a veterinarian. (By Thomas Rowlandson, Ride to Rumford, *reproduced from* Medicine and the Artist [Ars Medica] *by permission of the Philadelphia Museum of Art)*

RIDE TO RUMFORD
"Let the gall'd jade winch"

apothecary apprentices to attend lectures. Academic study started to be required in Italy in the late 18th century. And in the same period, some private pharmaceutical institutes were established in Germany. There some of the higher-class pharmacists attended university courses with physicians and surgeons.

The first full formal training for apothecaries was given at the College of Apothecaries, established in 1821 at the University of Pennsylvania in Philadelphia. Recognizing that the term "apothecary" was passing, it soon changed its name to the College of Pharmacy. The practice of formal education for pharmacists quickly spread in the United States, in Great Britain, and in continental Europe. Indeed, the first purely pharmaceutical research laboratories in history were established in England by two graduates of the Philadelphia College of Pharmacy.

In continental Europe, the result was that pharmacists retained their strong scientific orientation, now fortified by university training. Separated almost completely from physicians by the 19th century, some pharmacists continued to work as research scientists and to carry out or supervise medical laboratory work. Druggists, on the other hand, mostly unlicensed and untrained, dealt in the very wide nonprescription drug market.

In 19th-century England, however, apothecaries still provided considerable medical care. In that period, the apothecary was a kind of second-class physician, and many young men of good family but little means practiced as apothecaries in order to earn the money for medical training. Although physicians brought lawsuits against such apothecaries practicing medicine, they only won the judgment that apothecaries could give medical advice if they did not charge for it. Since apothecaries could and did include medical fees in their prescription charges, that posed no hardship, and they continued to practice as before. However, as modern medical training became more standardized, English apothecaries lost their independent identity and merged with physicians. The term "apothecary" effectively disappeared in England, and chemists and druggists combined to fill the former apothecary functions. They formed the Pharmaceutical Society of Great Britain in the mid-19th century. Later they introduced registration of qualified preparers of medicine, who thereafter were called pharmaceutical chemists, commonly shortened to "chemist."

Pharmacy in the United States continued to be relatively unregulated. Not only did American apothecaries generally follow the English model, practicing medicine and sometimes surgery as well, but egalitarian ideals encouraged the view that anyone should be free to practice the trade of his choice. During this period, many American pharmacists focused on sideline activities. One uniquely American sideline, the soda fountain, made the drugstore the center of social life in small towns for over a century. Pharmacists coming to the United States from France and Germany (especially after 1848) brought with them higher scientific standards. That and concern for consumer protection led to a gradual increase in government regulation.

In the late 19th century, trademarks played an important role in consumer protection, because pharmacists in many countries, especially in the United States, imported most of their drugs, either as finished products or in an intermediate state. Most large-scale manufacturing of pharmaceutical products, with medicines now ground by machine, was done in Germany. (This remained true until World War I spurred pharmaceutical production in other countries.) Since the consumer could not personally assess the skill and integrity of the producer, trademarks helped indicate the quality of the product, acting as a guard against products from unregulated or untrained drug suppliers. Such identification was not new. Long before the birth of Christ, apothecaries had been stamping a mark of origin on their products, and the use of trademarks had been regulated by the European pharmaceutical guilds. But, at a time when "patent medicines" pervaded every corner of North America, trademarks became especially important.

Historically, a patent was simply a monopoly granted to the seller of a particular remedy. It indicated nothing about the reliability or effectiveness of the medicine. Only in the 19th century did legislation give the term "patent" its modern meaning, that of a unique contribution, which in pharmacy could mean a new method of manufacture. It was not until later, when the production of drugs had become highly standardized, that many pharmaceutical trademarks ceased to perform an important function and primarily became selling devices used to make one company's product stand out from other similar products.

In the 20th century, the drug industry has come under increasingly heavy government regulation. Pharmaceutical firms, which sharply compete in finding new drugs and better marketing methods, have been forced to operate within scientific restraints, designed to ensure the effectiveness and safety of new drugs. Individual pharmacists, too, must operate under tighter restrictions,

Modern pharmacists buy much of their stock from large-scale manufacturers and, as always, supplement their incomes by selling a wide variety of other items, as in this late 19th-century drug store in Batavia, New York. (From Early Illustrations and Views of American Architecture, *by Edmund V. Gillon, Jr., Dover)*

intended to control access to certain types of medication except by physicians' prescriptions. The course of education for pharmacists has also expanded; most industrialized countries today require a five-year course leading to a bachelor of science degree in pharmacy, although some schools offer advanced master or doctoral programs. True to the double calling of the pharmacist, pharmaceutical programs stress the scientific courses that are similar to those given in the pre-medical curriculum, but also include business training. While women have always made up a small percentage of practicing pharmacists, their numbers have increased in the 20th century. By the late 1960s women made up over 20 percent of the students in American pharmacy schools; in some European countries the percentage was double that, while in the Soviet Union women predominate in modern pharmacy, as they do in the Soviet health-care system altogether.

Unregulated herb and drug sellers continue to operate in undeveloped countries and in many quarters of industrialized countries. Even though Western medical practices have been exported to many countries around the world and Western-style pharmacy has emerged, many people continue to prefer their traditional medicine. In such places, a "two-tier system" has developed, as has been common throughout the history of pharmacy. Alongside scientifically trained and regulated pharmacists are native apothecaries, who have come to be repositories of traditional regional medicine. This is true even in places like China, where such was not originally the apothecary's role. A similar process occurred when large numbers of immigrants moved from rural parts of the world to industrialized countries, notably in the early 20th century. They often brought their own apothecaries with them. Whether these apothecaries took scientific training and became licensed pharmacists or simply operated as importers of native herbs, they provided an alternative medical system for immigrant populations. In a way, the counterculture movements of the 1960s produced the same results. In rejecting much of the medical establishment, they opened the way for health-food stores and a host of unregulated medical advisers.

While the pharmacists have traditionally owned their own businesses, that pattern seems to be changing. Modern wholesaling of medications has given rise to drugstore chains, a development which first occurred in England and Scotland but which reached its full extension in the 20th-century United States. As 20th-century medical care has come to be centered in hospitals, many pharmacists have been employed in hospital pharmacies. Others have moved into pharmaceutical laboratories of large manufacturing firms or into service with large organizations, especially in those countries where national health services or substantial union health programs are operating. As a result, the pharmacist as an individual business owner of high standing is, in some countries, an endangered species, being replaced by the pharmacist-employee of a large company or service.

The roles of the pharmacist and the "second-tier" druggist are still very much in flux. They will probably continue to vary with changes in health-care systems and with differing national practices.

For related occupations in this volume, *Healers,* see the following:
    Barbers
    Dentists
    Nurses
    Physicians and Surgeons
    Veterinarians

For related occupations in other volumes of the series, see the following:
in *Harvesters:*
    Farmers
in *Restaurateurs and Innkeepers:*
    Costermongers and Grocers
in *Scholars and Priests:*
    Priests
    Monks and Nuns
    Teachers
in *Scientists and Technologists:*
    Alchemists
    Chemists

Physicians and Surgeons

The practice of medicine may date from as early as 30,000 B.C., perhaps even earlier. However, the oldest really hard evidence we have so far indicates that *surgeons* were at work in the late Neolithic period, between 10,000 and 7000 B.C.

This early surgical work included trepanning, or trephining, that is, cutting out a piece of the patient's skull; whether this was done to provide a hole for an evil spirit's escape or to ease pressure on the brain caused by injury or illness—both reasons given for such operations in historical times—is not clear. From the evidence of bone healing in prehistoric skulls found around the world, a significant portion of patients seem to have survived, indicating some skill on the part of these early surgeons, who used stone or bone tools. Early surgeons also seem to

The earliest known portrait of a physician may be this man, dressed in animal skins, from a painting over 15,000 years old in the Trois Frères cave in southern France.

have known how to set fractures and dislocations, perhaps temporarily packing the bones in place with earth or clay, later using splints and bandages for the same purpose.

Evidence for the practice of internal medicine is, of course, less clear. We know that *priest-physicians* functioned in Mesopotamia (modern Iraq) and elsewhere in Neolithic times, perhaps earlier. The man dancing in a stag's head mask, painted over 15,000 years ago on the wall of the Trois Frères cave in what is now southern France, suggests historic links between the *medicine man* of modern times and such a possible ancient counterpart. Whatever priest-physicians were called—*magicians, sorcerers, witch-doctors, spirit healers, medicine men, shamans*—they seem to have developed similar practices the world over. They relied heavily on chants and songs against demons and enemies; on charms for expelling diseases that were believed to have seized the body at the command of demons or as divine punishment; and on incantations to convey health, vigor, and long life to patients. In the absence of any scientific understanding of the causes of diseases, healers used magical tricks designed to fool or convince either demon or patient. Only gradually were other, more rational treatments added to the priest-physicians' practices.

Then, as now, most minor medical ailments were treated within the family. An elder person—often an old woman who may have been a *midwife,* but sometimes the male head of the family—was in charge of family or clan knowledge about herbal cures. But priest-physicians gradually became the specialists in herbal cures, and they were consulted for all serious ailments. Acting as their own *apothecaries (pharmacists),* they would very often personally harvest herbs, with appropriate incantations during the selection and picking, and prepare drugs for their patients. Other treatments that developed very early were massages, which sometimes took the form of trampling on the patient's body to persuade a demon to leave; sucking on a part of the patient's body to draw out an unwanted spirit, perhaps showing a pebble or wax pellet as evidence of success; and rubbing foul potions on the patient's body or giving them to the patient as a drink, to make the body unpleasant to the spiritual intruder. Such medical practices, with cultural variations, were widespread throughout the prehistoric world—and in some parts of the world they continue to be practiced today.

From the earliest times, priest-physicians had very high, sometimes godlike, status in their communities. Their practices were secret and were passed on only to selected successors, especially to sons of priest-physicians, generally through oral instruction. Pupils memorized the chants and treatments during their apprenticeship with the master. However as writing developed, priest-physicians in various cultures combined their knowledge and compiled written records of their medical rituals and practices. These practices included not only incantations but also practical techniques based on observation, although clouded with superstition. The earliest such written record of medical practices dates from around 3000 B.C. in Sumer, the Mesopotamian culture in which writing was first developed.

These records focused primarily on internal medicine, saying very little about surgery, for the Mesopotamians regarded surgery as a "lesser art" to be performed primarily by *barbers*. Their priest-physicians focused more on magical and drug therapies, practicing their art secretly in temples.

The first physicians we know by name were Egyptian: Sekhet'enanach, who was rewarded with a portrait in stone for having "healed the king's nostrils" around 3000 B.C., and Imhotep, who was also architect of the Step Pyramid at Saqqara, around 2900 B.C. Like the Sumerians, the Egyptians built up an extensive set of books on medical matters, which were sealed, to be read only by the priest-physicians. These books—all now lost, although some notes about them survive—outlined the methods of treatment to be used by the priest-physicians. In case of a patient's death, the physician would not be blamed as long as he had followed prescriptions in the books; otherwise he might be sentenced to death himself. The books were kept for reference in the temples—called the "houses of life"—and were carried by the priest-physicians in sacred processions.

Over the thousands of years during which Egyptian medicine was practiced, a medical hierarchy developed. At the top were the priests, or *wabw*. All priests were privileged to know the contents of the secret medical books and were able to examine patients, although not all had specific medical training or actually practiced medicine. Next came the lay physicians, who apparently treated the sick using both surgery and drugs. Their title—*swnw*—was formed by combining the symbols for knife and pot. Below them came the magicians, or *sa.u,* who worked only with charms. All these medical practitioners were assisted by *nurses, masseurs,* and other aides, many of whom were *slaves.* Some medical practitioners also acted as *veterinarians* for large or especially prized animals. (They would continue to do so even into modern times in areas where no animal specialists existed.) While most Egyptian medical practitioners

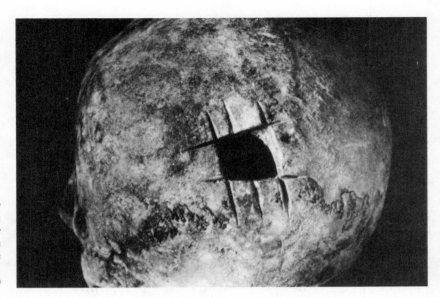

Early surgeons in many cultures performed an operation known as trepanning or trephining, in which a hole was cut in the patient's skull, as here. (Institute of Archaeology, University of London)

were men, one woman, Peneshet, became director of physicians. Other women were shown preparing drugs. Would-be physicians learned the medical writings by heart and attended consultations with priest-physicians.

Egyptian medicine was largely by and for the upper classes. In the "court of miracles" the high priest treated mostly wealthy people who made substantial offerings to the temples, as their fee to the physician. Later some physicians were attached to the royal courts and were paid salaries, instead of receiving fees for medical services; all physicians, however, charged for the medicines they provided. The division of medical labor in the Egyptian royal courts was extreme; for example, one pharaoh's physicians included "the keeper of the right eye" and "the keeper of the left eye."

The upper classes had the benefit of whatever treatments had been developed by the priest-physicians, such as particular diet and drug therapies. Bleeding—removal of blood from a patient, as by cutting a vein or attaching leeches—and enemas was among the treatments that the early Egyptians seem to have developed. Foul potions—including such substances as human urine, fly excrement, and crocodile dung (some of which did have antibiotic properties, whatever their adverse effects)—were part of the apothecary's store, along with herbal medicines, some from as far away as India and China. Early Egyptian physicians prepared their own drugs. Later some physicians had drugs prepared by apothecaries under their supervision.

Poorer patients were treated by a lesser class of physicians, the magicians. Patients would send a description of the illness to the temple and would be sent the appropriate magician to apply ancient treatments of incantations, amulets, and massage. Some physicians were also appointed to establish rules of public hygiene and to keep the thousands of workers fit for Egypt's massive building projects. Beyond that, the common people were largely ignored by the priest-physicians but were treated by self-appointed lay—that is, not professionally trained—healers and midwives.

In later times, Imhotep, the early physician credited with developing "temple sleep," became the symbol of Egyptian medicine. For this treatment, also called "incubation," a patient would come to the temple and be put to sleep with an herbal brew or drug, such as opium or henbane, along with some ritual incantations. The result was often a reviving rest for the patient. Egyptian priest-physicians elevated Imhotep first to a demigod and later to a full god in 500 B.C.—2500 years after his lifetime. He was worshipped well into the Christian era in the three temples devoted to him. The shell of one survived until the 1970s when it was flooded by the Aswan Dam.

Egyptian medicine drew patients from all over the Mediterranean. More important, Egyptian physicians were sent to provide special treatment in foreign courts as royal favors. Many physicians stayed as permanent advisers in Asia Minor (the land of the Hittites), Mesopotamia, Syria, and Persia.

Elsewhere in the Near East, Babylonia also developed a substantial class of physicians. Their ruler, Hammurabi, established codes of medical practice in 1800 B.C. regarding payment and punishment, both of which depended on the status of the patient. For example, the physician's fee for opening an eye abscess was 10 shekels for a nobleman, 2 shekels for a slave. The physician would lose his hands if a nobleman died or lost his sight during the operation; if the slave died, the physician needed only to provide a replacement. Such strong punishment—even if only threatened and not always carried out—may well have discouraged further developments in surgery in the Near East.

Among the Jews in these Old Testament times, physicians were not much favored and were barely mentioned in the Bible. God was regarded as the only source of disease or cure, and Asa in II Chronicles 12:12 was censured because "in his disease he sought not to the Lord but to the physicians." The relatively few remedies mentioned in the Bible come from "a man of God," and the only surgical procedure described was circumcision, which was usually performed by the priests. Instead of medical treatment, the Jews focused on public and social hygiene, codifying their practices into a set of dietary laws that were far ahead of their time and that, even today among orthodox Jews, maintain the old intertwining of health practices and religion.

Chinese Physicians

In the same period, the Chinese were developing quite a different system of medical thought and practice. As in other early cultures, the first physicians in China were medicine men or shamans—depicted in surviving clay figurines—who used magic and later drugs on their patients. To this they added techniques of massage, surgery, cautery (application of a hot surface, usually a branding iron, to burn clean and seal a wound), and bleeding. Although all these techniques were known and used in the Near East, the Chinese started to develop theories and practices of their own as early as 3000 B.C.

The belief that diseases resulted from imbalances between the *yin* and the *yang,* two opposing principles basic to much Chinese thought, dates from this early period. This theory gave rise to two techniques— moxibustion and acupuncture—designed to "remove" excess yin or yang and restore balance to the body. Moxibustion involves the burning of a small cone of wormwood, called a moxa, on the patient's skin. Often several moxas were burnt, in a geometric pattern, and the ashes crushed into the resulting blister. Acupuncture, which involves the insertion of needles at certain key points in the body, dates from as early as 2500 B.C.

As in other regions, the beginnings of medicine in China are enveloped in mythology. Most early discoveries are credited to three legendary Chinese figures—Fu Hsi (also called Pao Hsi), Shen Nung, and Huang Ti, all rulers between 3000 B.C. and 2600 B.C. Unnamed priest-physicians operating during this period must have made most, if not all, of these medical advances, for the work credited to these three rulers go far beyond what three individuals could accomplish in their lifetimes.

Some medical specialties were also developed. At the Chinese court were specialists in pulse, a main diagnostic tool for Chinese physicians. Other early priest-physicians developed new techniques of preparing and dispensing medicines, while early Chinese surgeons were said to have "cut skin, dissected muscles, severed blood vessels, tied tendons, and even washed the stomach and cleansed intestines."

The close association of physicians with the court was characteristic of China. Young men were often trained as civil servants first and physicians second, this approach holding true even up to modern times. By the 12th century B.C., the medical physicians at the court level had become separated from priests who made offerings and incantations for other purposes, such as to relieve droughts. However, priest-physicians continued to combine such functions for the general population.

This physician is taking his patient's pulse, one of the classic means of diagnosing an ailment in Chinese medicine. (Courtesy of the Wellcome Trustees, London)

In the eighth century B.C. China entered its golden age of medicine, and its historical records became more reliable. In an extensive series of written works, the Chinese described and classified diseases. Early Chinese physicians closely observed the physical characteristics of their patients. The pulse, for example, might be taken over a period of several hours; over 200 pulse variations were noted as indications of various imbalances or diseases. As a result of such observations and some surgical experience, the Chinese developed a partly accurate, partly imaginary understanding of anatomy and physiology. For example, they knew—2000 years before the English physician William Harvey made his discoveries about the circulatory system—that the heart regulated the blood flow, although they apparently had no idea of the operation of the arteries and veins. Similarly, they identified and named some main body organs, while leaving out others or inventing imaginary ones. With this mixture of knowledge, Chinese physicians began to develop prognoses—that is, forecasts of the course a patient's disease might take. They no longer assumed—as their earlier counterparts had done—that the disease resulted from supernatural intervention.

In this early period, the Chinese bureaucracy was already widespread and medical practitioners were part of it. Various categories of medical practitioners worked under the supervision of a chief physician. The highest ranking type of practitioner was the *dietician,* who selected and directed the preparation of the food and drink for patients, an indication of the importance of diet in early Chinese medicine. The second ranking category was the physician, who treated internal ailments. Below that was the surgeon, who tended to wounds, broken bones, and external sores, such as abscesses and ulcers. Finally came the *veterinarians,* who cared for animals. The chief physician and his staff kept careful records; the medical staff was promoted or demoted—and had their annual salary fixed—according to their percentage of successful treatments. Medical officers were also posted to prisons and institutions for the handicapped or insane, which were primarily shelters, not hospitals in the modern sense.

The greatest period of Chinese medicine was the Han dynasty, which lasted from two centuries before to two centuries after the birth of Christ. The achievements in Chinese medicine at this time are exemplified by China's three greatest physicians. The first, Ts'ang Kung, developed the procedure of taking case histories. Unfortunately, although his students continued the practice for a short time, such record keeping died out for almost 1000 years. The second, Chang Ching, a highly influential medical writer, was expert in a wide variety of treatments and drugs. He also paid close attention to the physical signs and symptoms of illnesses and is credited with introducing the enema as a treatment in China. The third was Hua T'o, later worshipped as a god of surgery, who performed a wide range of operations, using various narcotics as at least partial anesthetics. He also introduced to China the use of hydrotherapy (water treatment) to reduce fever. A few women physicians operated in this period as well, treating primarily female patients.

Even at this height of Chinese medicine, however, most physicians were accorded only low status, akin to that of artisans. The Chinese considered medicine part of a basic Confucian education, required of a well-born son so he could care for his relatives, especially his parents. But medical practice itself was frowned upon. As Confucius said, "A scholar is not an instrument." Many Confucians did earn livelihoods by practicing medicine, especially those who failed their civil service examinations, but the Chinese view of such practitioners was expressed in the common sentiment that "he who does not work as a [government] minister, can at least work as a physician."

Not surprisingly, since Confucians had no practical training, many other types of physicians developed, among them hereditary practitioners, who carried on family medical practices that were handed down from generation to generation. A patient did not have one regular doctor but consulted several physicians in turn. The physician came only when called and was not expected to call again to check on the patient's progress; that was considered primarily the family's responsibility. Many operated in public places and drew large crowds, while others made contracts for cures, took the money for treatment, and then ran away in order to avoid being blamed for failures. Chinese physicians acted as their own apothecaries, gathering and preparing drugs. But some medical writers advised that the physician should leave even the preparation of drugs—especially those with expensive ingredients—to the family, to avoid being accused of cheating. The eldest son would, in any event, taste the medicine, to see that it was not poisonous, before giving it to his parents.

Warring medical factions contributed to the decline of Chinese medicine from its promising advances in the Han Dynasty. The dominant Confucians regarded the independent physicians—who were often the only ones with practical experience—with contempt. That view was widely held by patients as well (although they also feared that the Confucian physicians, regardless of their status, had little useful knowledge for healing illnesses). Surgery virtually died out in China, mutilation of the body being forbidden by Confucians in later periods. From the end of the Han Dynasty in 220 A.D., medical practice became increasingly overlaid with philosophical theories and divorced from practical observation. China fell into a medical dark age.

Indian Physicians

In between Egypt and China was another major cultural area. The highly developed Indus Valley civilization, which traded with both Egypt and China, was conquered by Aryan (Indo-European) tribes from the north around 1500 B.C. After a period of turmoil, these two cultures merged and produced a flowering of Indian medicine. This is recorded in the *Vedas,* early sacred records written in the Aryan language, Sanskrit, which became the language of the priests.

Indian medicine was at first largely magical, relying heavily on charms and incantations. But Indian physicians very early began to supplement these with medicines and, while retaining a magical cast to their writing and treatments, developed a surprisingly rational medical system. They focused on clinical histories and close observation of the patient's symptoms, rather than relying solely on a book of prescriptions to dictate treatment, as the Egyptians did. They developed a wide range of diagnoses, not assuming that all diseases with similar symptoms were the same. For example, they recognized 20 different kinds of earaches, and they developed considerable skill in dealing with various poisonous snakebites, which were common in subtropical India. In addition, they recognized that mosquitos caused malaria and that plague followed when rats died; they seem to have even practiced inoculation against smallpox.

Even more remarkable, these early Indians developed great skill in surgery, employing some techniques not known elsewhere until the 19th century. The earliest medical records do not mention surgery, and it seems likely that surgical techniques were originally developed by a separate group of practitioners. The Hindu word for surgery is *salya*, meaning "arrow," which may indicate that the earliest of these were wound surgeons who accompanied battle troops. But by the first century A.D., surgery had become fully united with medicine in India. Indian physicians tended to treat the whole patient, rather than dividing responsibility according to different body parts, as did the Egyptians, or leaving surgery to supposed inferiors, as did the Mesopotamian peoples. The early physician Susruta put it this way: "He who knows only one branch of his art is like a bird with one

Aryan or Indo-European surgeons carried with them bags of herbs and implements as they moved into India, much like this surgeon, depicted on a Phoenician vase found in Russia. (From Vincenzo Guerini's A History of Dentistry)

wing." Hindu physicians, using over 120 different instruments and various narcotics, especially alcohol, practiced all the surgical techniques known before modern times, except ligature, which is used to stop hemorrhaging (uncontrolled bleeding). They performed internal operations to remove tumors or foreign objects, lancing or puncturing to drain collected fluid or abscesses, and cleansing and stitching internal wounds. Three operations seem to have been developed first by the Indians: lateral lithotomy, that is, removal of a stone from the bladder; plastic surgery, which involved transplanting a flap of skin to an amputated area, often the nose, which was commonly removed as a punishment for such crimes as adultery; and repair of anal fistula, which is an abnormal opening in the rectum.

Indian physicians also developed a unique method of anatomical dissection, at a time when autopsies were forbidden in most cultures, including the Hindu one. Physicians were not allowed to touch anything that might contaminate them, a religious prohibition that was probably linked to the rapidity of decomposition in the warm, moist Indian climate. To circumvent this objection, Indian physicians would wrap a corpse in a bag of woven grasses and place it in a secluded backwater along a river for a week, at the end of which time the blood would have leached out and the body would be "cleansed." Then, without touching the body directly, physicians would use delicate bamboo brushes to scrape away layers of flesh, uncovering the structures underneath much as modern archeologists uncover successive layers at ancient sites. While such dissections were never widely performed—and knowledge from them was limited—the Indians still gained an understanding of anatomy unparalleled in the ancient world.

The Indians were also remarkable in developing very early a rational approach to sickness. Rather than assuming that illness or failure of medical treatment was caused by supernatural forces, they developed a four-question approach they applied to the patient. First, is the patient ill, or does he only seem so? Second, if ill, what is the sickness and its source? Third, can the physician cure the disease? (If not, the proper response was deemed to be withdrawal, leaving the patient in the hands of family and priest.) Finally, if the illness is treatable, what treatment is indicated? Among the diseases the Indians regarded as treatable were fever, diarrhea, cough, consumption, sores, and abscesses. Whatever treatment was recommended by the physician, however, religious devotion and yoga practice were also considered necessary to bring about the well-being of the whole person.

As in Egypt, medicine in India was practiced primarily by the upper classes. The early medical writers Charaka and Susruta both expressed the ideal that medicine should be studied only by the three highest classes of Indian society. The *Brahmins,* the priestly classes, were supposed to cure without charge all who needed their help; the *Ksattriya,* the feudal aristocracy, were supposed to treat themselves; and the *Vaisya,* the tradespeople and skilled laborers, were actually to practice medicine as a profession. While training for the Brahmins involved somewhat more ceremony and ritual, medical training was similar for all three groups, generally beginning when students were 12 years old. In a ceremony similar to a wedding, students were bonded to a master, with whom they would live for at least six years, while they learned the art and craft of medicine.

Book-learning, practical assistance, and observation of the master were the methods by which students were taught. They were required to memorize the complete medical texts of the time. But the masters were convinced that memorization alone did not make a fine physician; they insisted that pupils also become adept at all practical skills. Students learned how to handle all surgical instruments by using them on practice objects. Incisions and amputations were practiced on cucumbers or melons, for example, and wound-stitching was practiced with soft leather and thread.

Indian physicians were all male, as were most of their

patients. Women and children—except royalty and Brahmin pregnant women—were left largely in the hands of uneducated midwives. Physicians were required to be young, healthy, full of stamina, clean, and self-controlled. In addition, keen senses were extremely important; in the absence of scientific means of analysis, the physician most often relied on physical observation, including the taste of a patient's bodily secretions, in diagnosis of ailments. Indian physicians had very high status, and some physicians from lower classes were able to raise their social status by virtue of excellence in their profession; all were exempted from taxes, a clear indication of the community's view of their importance. The highest-ranking physicians were those associated with the court. They sat at the right hand of their princes and examined those who had completed medical training.

Despite the belief that Brahmins should use their medical knowledge to alleviate the sufferings of all, the poor in early India generally had to rely on wandering folk healers for their medical care. As part of the Buddhist "reformation," however, the ideal became somewhat more of a reality. Believing that good works were the way to Nirvana (heaven), wealthy and noble Buddhists began to establish hospitals all across India for the poor (and also for animals). These well-constructed, attractive hospitals had trained staffs headed by physicians, and they were surrounded by their own specially planted gardens of herbs. In the third century B.C., Asoka, emperor of the Mauryan Dynasty, noted that Buddhist hospitals provided medical care for people and animals from Ceylon (now Sri Lanka) to Persia (Iran) and Syria.

Indian physicians also developed a code of ethics, which included an injunction to "dedicate yourself entirely to helping the sick, even though this be at the cost of your own life," and a caution not to speak to others about anything observed in the patient's house. The date of this Indian oath is uncertain, but it is strikingly similar to the Hippocratic Oath developed in Greece. Indeed, the relationship between Indian medicine and Greek medicine, which also experienced a golden age in the centuries before Christ, is complicated. Given contacts between the two civilizations in that period, borrowings from each other seem likely, but the true extent of mutual influence is unclear.

Greek Physicians

While the Aryans were building a golden age of medicine in India, their Indo-European kin were establishing the basis for the first truly scientific medicine—quite separate from religion—in the world. Moving southward from western Asia, the people we know as the Greeks conquered and merged with the native populations of Greece, the Ionian islands, and the coastal regions of Asia Minor. Like the Aryans, the battling Greeks seem to have had a group of surgeons traveling with their armies. These surgeons focused on practical wound care and application of drugs, without any mystical or religious trappings. In fact, far from being priests with high status, these wandering surgeons had the status of workers in the manual trades; they were called *demiourgoi,* meaning "men who work for the people."

Greek medicine was the successor to earlier traditions, drawing upon not only Egyptian and Babylonian cultures but also possibly from Indian and even Chinese sources. It is no accident that the centers of Greek medicine were on and near the coast of Asia Minor, the crossroads of the main trade routes with the Near and Far East.

Greek centers of medical education were not formal schools as we know them, but informal groupings of masters of medicine, who joined together to share knowledge and theories. Around them gathered students who wished to learn the medical art. A student paid an agreed-upon fee to a master and thereafter followed his master on his rounds, learning from both oral instruction and practical experience. Apprentices

One of the early Greek surgeons was the perhaps-mythical Iapyx, here shown removing an arrow from the thigh of Trojan hero Aeneas. (From a fresco in Pompeii, Museo Archeologico Nazionale, Naples)

were often used as assistants, helping to prepare drugs, assisting in operations, and watching over recuperating patients (in that respect becoming the first trained nurses in the West). No medical licensing existed; anyone who could pay the fee could apprentice himself to a physician and, when he chose, then go out on his own as a physician—anyone except women, who were barred from such activity in Greece. Medical schools were often associated with other schools of philosophy and science and, as medicine partook of each, it too became part of the general education of many Greeks. Some philosophers studied medicine without practicing it, and their interest raised the social status of the medical art.

By the sixth century B.C., the practice of internal and external medicine had become the domain of one type of medical person, the *iatros,* (healer). Many healers continued to operate as wanderers. Like artisans, they often worked in open-sided booths off market squares; examinations and operations were often done in full view of the street. Often several physicians might work in the same marketplace. The patient could choose among medical competitors, who would sometimes heckle each other in the battle for patients, giving medical treatment at times the aura of a sideshow. The physician's apprentices, assistants, or slaves would treat aliens and other slaves. Many other physicians, mostly well-born Greeks or educated foreigners residing in Greek cities, developed more permanent followings. They would work out of their homes, possibly housing some patients during recuperation. The upper classes were treated in their own homes.

Some physicians came to be so valued that they were hired as *municipal physicians* and paid salaries that were raised from citizens by special taxes. Such physicians were to treat free of charge all who came to them. The first municipal physician we know by name is Democedes, son of a physician from Croton. He was physician to the city of Aegina and later to Athens and Samos.

Oddly enough, religion seems to have entered Greek medicine by the back door. As physicians began to have higher status, being linked more with philosophers than artisans—and perhaps also in imitation of the Egyptian deification of Imhotep in Egypt—the Greek physicians adopted as their patron or hero Asclepius, the mythical son of Apollo, god of healing. As early as the sixth century B.C., shrines and temples were being erected in his honor, one of the first being established at Epidaurus. Asclepius proved to be a popular hero. In the next two centuries, Asclepian temples spread throughout the Greek world, to Athens, the island of Cos, and the cities of Asia Minor, and from there even farther around the Mediterranean. In all, over 400 Asclepian temples were founded. Although originally adopted as the patron of secular physicians, Asclepius gradually came to be worshipped as a god. His worship formed the basis for an alternate Greek medical system with a strong religious and mystical foundation.

In the many temples in his honor around the Mediterranean, the physician-god Asclepius is often shown accompanied by his daughter Hygeia, goddess of healing, as here. (National Archaeological Museum, Athens)

The temples in which Asclepius was worshipped, along with his two daughters, the goddesses Hygeia and Panacea, seem to have been modeled after the Egyptian temples of incubation. Not hospitals in the modern sense, they were more like modern health resorts—built on beautiful hilly sites, often associated with baths, gymnasiums, gardens, and theaters. A patient came to the Asclepian temple, having perhaps fasted before arrival; took a purifying bath and a massage, thereafter being wrapped in a white gown; made a sacrifice or left a gift on the altar; then was given a sleep-inducing herbal brew to drink and was laid to sleep on an open porch (men were on one side of the building and women on the other) with soothing music playing and scented smoke wafting through the air. The temple priest-physician, dressed like Asclepius and accompanied by a group of assistants, would come to the sleeping patient "in a dream" and give Asclepius's counsel, sometimes also performing a minor operation. Sacred snakes, which were thought to have special healing powers, were sometimes placed with the patients while they slept. These snakes, or sometimes dogs, were placed in such a way that they would lick the affected area. Asclepius and his followers, in fact, were often pictured with snakes over their shoulders; the modern medical symbol of two serpents twined around a staff (a caduceus) apparently derives from this connection. In the morning the patient would arise and go home, although some might stay for a few days. Walls of the surviving Asclepian temples record many cures—and no failures or deaths. This remarkable string of successes, however, owes a great deal to patients' expectations of being cured, and even more to the selection process—no seriously ill patients or pregnant women were accepted.

As in Egypt, offerings to the temple were the priest-physicians' fees. Patients' fees varied with their ability to pay, and payment was sometimes extended over a period of time. Priests would threaten to "revoke" the cure if payments were not made. Asclepian physicians did, however, provide some free medical care to the poor, even into the Christian era. Indeed, Asclepian practices later merged in some areas with faith-healing practices of early Christians. Even into the 20th century, when the temples of Asclepius had been closed for many centuries, sick people were sometimes taken to spend the night in a church in parts of Greece and on some of the eastern Mediterranean islands.

Asclepius captured the popular fancy—many people thought of all physicians as Asclepian healers—but the major advances in Greek medicine were really made by secular physicians. In line with the Greek philosophers who sought reasonable, not supernatural, explanations of events, secular physicians assumed that patients were not sinful, but sick. They also assumed that disease was not a single entity with many symptoms, as many physicians previously had thought, but that there were many diseases with different symptoms and causes. They set themselves to observing and recording the critical signs and stages of the diseases they treated, developing clinical histories. They developed and used many of the same surgical techniques known to Indian physicians, although, without the same systematic practical training, they did not achieve as high a general level of skill. In addition, they developed the techniques of ligature, that is, tying off the ends of blood vessels to prevent hemorrhaging during surgery, and of podalic version, in which a mis-oriented child would be turned in its mother's womb so that it could be born in the normal head-down position.

The writings of the most important secular physicians were later collected, and many of them came to be associated with Hippocrates, a physician from the island of Cos. Writings attributed to Hippocrates were not collected until some years after his death, so it is not clear which were indeed written by him or under his direct influence and which were the works of other physicians. But together these writings set the standards for Greek secular medicine, and Hippocrates became the symbol of the ideal physician.

Of all these writings, the best known is the Hippocratic Oath which, in various versions, is still used as part of the graduation ceremony of many medical schools. This oath was not unique; it drew on secret oaths and commitments made by physicians (and priests) earlier and elsewhere, such as in Egypt and India. Indeed the oath itself may have originated in the school of Pythagoras, not being a practical guide actually followed but an attempt to raise the standard of medical conduct and to counter the unscrupulous activities of some physicians. Physicians taking the oath promised to do no harm to their patients, to protect the privacy of patients, to honor their teachers,

The depiction of medical treatment was a popular subject in ancient Greek art and sculpture. (National Archaeological Museum, Athens)

and to pass on their learning to their sons and the sons of their teachers.

After the time of Hippocrates, as the Greek world expanded around the Mediterranean, the Egyptian port of Alexandria became the center of the medical world. In about 300 B.C., a major medical school was founded there, with substantial laboratories and an affiliation with Alexandria's world-famous library. At that library were brought together in one place manuscripts of all that was known of medical training in the Western world of the time. The best scientific and medical talents gathered there, and Alexandria provided by far the most systematic medical training of its time. Students from all over the Mediterranean aspired to study at Alexandria; to have done so made many a physician's career. The fame of Alexandria, building on both Greek and Egyptian traditions, was so great that, centuries later, the Greco-Roman physician Galen noted that a physician would never go amiss in sprinkling a few Egyptian words into a prescription. As late as the 18th century, outright charlatans were still selling "mummy powder direct from Egypt" to the gullible who wished to purchase "immortality."

One of the major innovations in Alexandria was the practice of anatomical dissection. Because dissection had been forbidden by so many civilizations, most early physicians had virtually no knowledge of anatomy other than what they might learn by analogy from sacrificing animals and tending wounded patients. At Alexandria, however, anatomists went to the other extreme: They carried out dissections of the living. Herophilus, perhaps the first person to do a public dissection of a human body, about 300 B.C., and his colleague, Erasistratus, are reported to have dissected the live bodies of over 600 people, all criminals supplied for the purpose by royal permission. Most of what was learned of anatomy in such operations was, however, lost in the later destruction of the library of Alexandria, and of other medical libraries elsewhere in the Classical world.

Physicians in Rome

As the political lead passed from the Greeks to the Romans, physicians began gravitating toward Rome. The early Romans had no formal medical practitioners. The head of each family was responsible for the family members' good health, which he ensured by making appropriate sacrifices and using herbal medicines passed down through the generations. However, in 293 B.C. Rome was hit by a plague, which none of the traditional Roman methods could counter, so according to the Roman historian Livy, Romans sought help from Greek Asclepian temples.

After the Romans conquered the Greeks in 146 B.C., Greek medicine spread to Rome, the new political and social center of the Mediterranean. Because the Romans had no independent medical traditions, their physicians were all foreigners—mostly Greeks but some Egyptians and Jews—considered to be social inferiors by the Romans. Many of these early physicians were slaves, whose fees were paid to their masters; but eventually most were allowed to buy their freedom. Medicine later came to be more highly respected in Rome, especially when surgeons were needed to care for the many soldiers who were wounded in battle campaigns. In 46 B.C. Julius Caesar granted full Roman citizenship to all medical practitioners and, when all other foreigners were expelled from Rome that year during a serious famine, Greek physicians were allowed and encouraged to stay.

Early Rome had no general hospitals. Most people were treated at home, in shops near market squares, or in rooms attached to the physician's home, which came to be called the *iatreia*. Old and sick slaves were sent to an island in the Tiber where an Asclepian temple stood, but they were not treated, only "exposed" and left to die of starvation. (Emperor Claudius decreed that any slaves who recovered after being placed on the island should go free and need not return to their masters.) Nor did soldiers have any hospital care in earlier Roman times;

sick or wounded soldiers were simply lodged in the homes of citizens until their recovery. In Caesar's time, military hospitals began to be built in strategic places, especially around the rim of the empire. Wounded or ill soldiers could be sent there for treatment and recuperation. These hospitals—the only ones in Europe at the time—were spacious, well-supplied, and well-built, although unadorned. To keep the hospitals well-staffed, the Emperor Vespasian (69-79 A.D.) established state-supported medical schools, providing training for those who wished it. Military physicians were given noncommissioned officer rank, were freed from combat duty, and, unlike soldiers, were allowed to marry while in service. Physicians were also assigned to most ships, at double pay and rations.

As Greek medicine came to be appreciated, and as Greek habits came to be fashionable in Rome, the physician's status rose. Some physicians counted among their friends Mark Antony and Cicero, along with other highly regarded Roman citizens. The Emperor Augustus rewarded his personal physician, a Greek freedman named Musa, with a statue and a noble title; and in 10 A.D. Augustus exempted all physicians from taxes. A century later, under the Emperor Hadrian, physicians were freed of civic duties and military service, and were allowed to move freely to more promising locations within the empire. In this century, too, Romans ceased their disapproval of practicing professions for gain, and for the first time physicians—Romans called them *medici*—were drawn from the ranks of Roman citizens. In the process, medicine gained equal status with other professions, such as law.

Physicians trained in the fine medical schools of the eastern Mediterranean found these conditions attractive and headed for Rome. In this period, top physicians and surgeons vied for lucrative institutional positions; *medici* were appointed to most major institutions, such as gladiatorial amphitheatres, and government divisions, such as cities or community districts. Such positions

This Roman physician is shown examining the eyes of a woman patient. (Musée Barrois, Bar-le-Duc)

carried high rank and special privileges, as well as generally benefiting private practices. Most important of these official physicians was the *archiater,* a term originally reserved for the Roman emperor's personal physician but later applied to the chief physician of any institution or department.

Unfortunately, the flow of physicians to Rome did not raise the level of medical care available to the general population of the Roman Empire. Many physicians moved to Rome, leaving their home areas with little or no medical care. Shortages of physicians in some areas became so great that regulations were modified. A *medicus* moving from his original home, for example, would lose his privileges unless he was granted the right to move because of his reputation. Another serious problem in major Roman centers was the influx of untrained quacks, often specializing in a single treatment or part of the body. Until 200 A.D., Rome had no medical licensing laws, no state supervision, and no educational requirements. Even after that, as was true in earlier Greece, to be a doctor you needed only to call yourself one—and attract patients. Some self-proclaimed physicians were better at public relations than at medicine; a few even boasted that they could train anyone to be a physician in just six weeks. The problem of finding a qualified physician was further complicated by the disintegration of medicine into rival cults that competed for public approval.

While medicine in the Roman Empire was declining into theoretical disputation and quackery, the famous physician Galen made a major contribution to medicine by preserving the best of Greek medicine. Reportedly keeping 12 scribes busy during his preparation of over 500 books, he detailed all that he had learned about medicine, in effect summarizing the medical knowledge of the Mediterranean world. In doing so, he also recorded the errors of his time, including his own, especially in the area of anatomy. Dissection was no longer allowed in the Roman world. Except for one human cadaver, all Galen's anatomical dissections had been of animals; unfortunately, that led him to record a number of anatomical mistakes.

The importance of Galen's work was magnified over the centuries, as the Mediterranean world underwent some major changes. In the fourth century, Christianity was adopted as the state religion of the Roman Empire, and all things regarded as pagan were ordered to be destroyed. That included many medical institutions and records, because the early Christians felt that medicine was closely tied to pagan religion (as indeed some of it still was) and believed that Christ was the only healer.

Medical and surgical techniques developed by the Greeks, and refined and spread under the Romans, survived in the Eastern Roman Empire, as in this 11th-century method of readjusting the spinal column. (Biblioteca Medicea-Laurenziana, Florence)

When, in the next two centuries, the western half of the Roman Empire collapsed altogether, with it went whatever remaining institutions had passed on medical knowledge in an orderly way.

Some medical writings did survive this debacle, especially in the eastern part of the empire, where medical practice went on, although completely stagnated. More important, some of these writings were taken farther east by refugees fleeing the Roman Christian world. In the fifth century, Bishop Nestorius of Constantinople—accused of heresy and excommunicated from the Christian church—immigrated to the Near East with many of his followers (some of whom went on into Central Asia and China). In the same century many Greek philosophers, leaving Athens after the Academy was closed, settled in Persia, especially in the city of Gundishapur. There they found the descendants of many Jews who had fled the Roman destruction of Jerusalem in 76 A.D. as well as descendants of Greek physicians who had followed Alexander the Great, over six centuries earlier. Many of these refugee scholars took with them manuscripts of the ancient world in Greek, Roman, Syrian, and Hebrew; these would later provide a basis for a resurgence of medicine.

But in Europe, medicine was disintegrating. With faith healing on the rise, scientific medical practice fell into disfavor; many physicians moved into other lines of work. The remaining physicians passed medical knowledge on orally to the few apprentices who worked with them. Unfortunately, in the absence of organized schools and written works, much medical knowledge was lost in transmission. Since few physicians had an overview of medicine, the result was a fragmenting of medical practice. Each physician operated with the knowledge and skill he had at his disposal; many specialized in one particular technique, such as eye surgery or lithotomy (cutting a stone from the bladder or urethra). In this period, medical practitioners generally reverted to being rough, often wandering artisans, as they had been in early Greece.

In the late fourth century, the Christian church did begin to develop infirmaries to care for the sick, poor, disabled, and homeless, but these had very little to do with medicine. Lay people, priests, and nurses ran these hospices, which mainly provided food, shelter, and religious counsel. Physicians were only occasionally called in as consultants, and their advice was often ignored. Indeed, in these early religious hospices, prescriptions were very often religious rather than medical. It was not uncommon, for example, for a priest to prescribe that a patient drink a cup of herbal tea into which had been stirred the ashes of a burnt Paternoster (a sheet of paper on which had been written the prayer beginning "Our Father who art in Heaven"). Many priests were, in essence, faith healers; in some areas "Christ the healer" cults merged with older Asclepian cults, Christ subsituting for Asclepius. Despite their religion's disapproval of medicine, some early Christian physicians continued to practice their increasingly limited art. Later when the church once more embraced medical healing, some were made saints. Among these were St. Luke the Evangelist, whom St. Paul called "the beloved physician," and two Arab Christian brothers, Cosmas and Damian, martyred by the Emperor Diocletian in the early fourth century and later made the patron saints of medicine and pharmacy, respectively.

In the period after the fall of the Western Roman Empire in the fifth century, the relatively few surviving classical records were collected and preserved in monastery and abbey libraries, where they were laboriously copied and recopied. Among these records were medical works, but—the church still being ambivalent about medicine—knowledge preserved from earlier times was seldom applied to actual patient care in the hospices. For example, one of the main collections of medical manuscripts was found in the great Benedictine abbey at Monte Cassino, Italy; although the monks there spent considerable time transcribing medical manuscripts, the founder of the order, St. Benedict, forbade his followers to practice medicine in this early period, believing that cures could only come through faith. In this way, medical care in Europe languished during the darkest of the Dark Ages.

Medieval Asia

But while medicine in Europe was being dismembered, the medicine of India and China was still vital and spreading throughout Asia. In India, the earlier apprenticeship system had been supplemented by the establishment of some major medical schools, notably at Benares on the Ganges and at Taxila in northwest India, dedicated to teaching "the wisdom of life," which was medicine. This high Indian medical skill traveled, with Buddhist missionaries, to Ceylon, Indonesia, Tibet, Japan, and even to China. In many of these places it flourished. In the fourth century A.D., Ceylon was reported to have had a widespread network of Buddhist hospitals, with a physician for every 10 villages. The decline in Buddhism in India after the seventh century and, later, the takeover by the Moslem culture caused the Indian hospital system to disintegrate in its homeland, but it still thrived in many other parts of southeast Asia. In Ceylon, large Buddhist hospitals were still operating in the 12th century A.D. Traveling surgeons used Indian techniques in Asia and in Europe for many centuries.

Farther east, the dominant influence in medicine was China. Along with Chinese writing and culture, Chinese medicine spread to surrounding countries, primarily between the third and ninth centuries, largely replacing the traditional medical practices of those regions. China itself continued to have a strong bureaucratic system for scholars. In the early seventh century, state medical colleges were established in the main Chinese cities; for the first time prospective physicians there were expected to pass qualifying examinations before being allowed to practice. Students came from all over China as well as from nearby countries, such as Japan. Distinguished from other citizens by a special cap and belt, they studied at the colleges, taking tests each month and quarter, before entering practice on their own. Medical teachers were responsible for their students' performances, being fined or demoted if their students did not do well on the

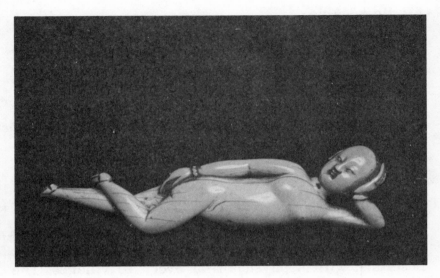

In Early China, women marked the site of their ailment on carved ivory figurines like these, rather than be examined by a male physician. (Courtesy of the Wellcome Trustees, London)

examinations; graduate physicians were slotted into the medical hierarchy according to the test results. Unfortunately, since most such students were destined for careers as court physicians, these medical colleges did little to advance the general level of medical care provided in East Asia.

Throughout China, a wide variety of other healers continued to operate. The split between intellectual and manual work continued, with educated Confucian physicians still disdaining practical experience and many other practitioners lacking the benefit of book-learning. Both types of physicians saw the actual practice of collecting a fee for medical advice as degrading; they worked for fees, nevertheless.

Monks and nuns in Buddhist and Taoist hospitals served the general population for several centuries, but in the seventh century they were forbidden to practice medicine; the hospitals were secularized and then allowed to degenerate by the Confucians, who were jealous of rival religious institutions. As in many other early cultures, the physician's home often became a small hospital, where patients recuperated. In later centuries, a few women doctors also operated. This was a boon for female patients, for modesty dictated that male physicians not examine or often even see a woman. Instead, physicians carried with them diagnostic figures, small carved statues on which the woman would indicate the site of the ailment; some high-born women had their own elaborately decorated figures to send to a physician by messenger.

The medical bureaucracy continued to exist in China into modern times, but gradually it disintegrated into a series of rival schools and cults, each with its own theories about causes and treatments of diseases. Medical thinking and practice stagnated, and qualifying examinations were often disregarded, so many untrained and incompetent physicians were appointed.

Physicians in the Moslem World

While medicine declined in Europe and India, and fragmented and stagnated in China, it flourished in the Moslem or Islamic world. The medical literature brought by refugee scholars from the Roman Christian world was eagerly translated and studied by the scholars of the Moslem Near East. As Islam—the religion of Mohammed—expanded, starting in the seventh century, copies of these manuscripts accompanied the conquerors into their new territories. Like the Greeks before them, the Moslems built upon the base of earlier learning, providing a congenial home for some of the best scientific minds of the time. Although they had no scientific tradition of their own, the Moslems welcomed and protected Christian and Jewish scientists, especially physicians; even Mohammed's personal physician was a non-Moslem. Gradually native Arab physicians emerged to join them, including two of the greatest Moslem medical teachers: Rhazes, born in the ninth century, and Avicenna, born a century later. Being from Persia, both of these scholar-physicians drew not only on the learning of the Mediterranean world, but also on the traditions of India, which was later brought under Moslem rule, possibly taking from China as well.

Over the centuries, especially from the 10th to the mid-12th centuries, the Moslems built an elaborate medical system. In their great cities, notably Cairo, Alexandria, Damascus, Gundishapur, and Baghdad, they built medical centers, including libraries, lecture rooms, apothecary shops, and hospitals. These hospitals had gardens, music, and storytellers for the patients, as had Indian hospitals and Greek temples before them—and the cuisine was so good that people sometimes faked illness to enter the hospital. The hospitals were set up in modern fashion, with separate wards for different types of illnesses. (In contrast, infirmaries in medieval Europe had open wards, with patients—some ill, some simply old or poor—placed together indiscriminately, two or three to a bed.) Like most earlier cultures, the Moslems forbade dissection; they also disapproved of surgery unless absolutely necessary. As an alternative, they developed a wide range of cauterizing techniques. In addition, they made significant advances in preparing and standardizing drugs, which were shipped by caravan to many parts of the world.

Physicians were trained at Moslem medical centers and, beginning in the ninth century, they and pharmacists were required to pass examinations before being licensed to practice. (Possibly the Moslems were inspired in this by the Chinese system of qualifying examinations.) The training focused on clinical observations and medical histories, in the tradition of the Hippocratic school, without a heavy overlay of religious dogma. Unlicensed healers continued to work, however. Midwives treated most women; if a male physician was called in, the female patient and midwife generally consulted him through a heavy curtain, in accordance with the cultural seclusion of women. In addition, there was a class of street doctors and lay healers who provided medical care to the poor or gullible and who—as elsewhere—continued to practice despite attempts to control them in the 10th century and later.

Along with a growing body of scientifically based medical knowledge, the Moslems also developed elaborate techniques in areas destined to be, on balance, scientific dead ends: astrology, uroscopy, and alchemy. Astrology pervaded the Middle Ages, and astrologers were consulted not only at the birth of a patient, but also at the onset of an illness, to determine which planet was governing the affected part of the body. Uroscopy, the analysis of urine, was used as a primary method of diagnosis. Physicians had to follow elaborate charts and tables developed in the Moslem medical centers. (Urine analysis is important in medicine today, but this medieval study had little or no relation to modern scientific analysis.) Alchemy was the attempt to produce gold from "baser" metals, part of a wider attempt to find the secret of long life and even immortality; metals and crushed jewels were used for this purpose, along with substances having medicinal properties.

Europe's Medical Revival

Moslem medical learning—the scientific and the superstitious—gradually made its way into Christian Europe. The textbooks of Rhazes and Avicenna eventually came to dominate European medical education, along with about 80 surviving works of Galen and some revived works of Hippocrates, until the 17th century. The process began early. In 639 A.D., less than a decade after Mohammed's death, the Moslems established a medical school at Córdoba, Spain; in time, Córdoba grew to have over 500 hospitals, 17 universities, and a library of more than 100,000 medical manuscripts. To Córdoba and other medical centers came students from around the Moslem world, and even a few from Europe. Some graduates later practiced in Christian Europe.

Jewish physicians were especially important in spread-

Among the special skills that survived during the medieval period was the cataract eye operation here being performed by an Arabic physician. (World Health Organization, Geneva)

ing the science that had developed in the Moslem centers. Although many remained to work in the Moslem world, some set up practice elsewhere in Europe. Jewish physicians in many Christian areas were allowed by law to practice only in Jewish ghettos; Christians were forbidden to employ them; and Jewish physicians were subject to severe penalties for treating Christian patients. But Jewish doctors trained in the great Moslem centers like Córdoba were widely recognized as the best physicians, and the noble and the rich—including the high Catholic clergy—often consulted them secretly. The spread of medical learning was spurred even further when, in the 12th century, Moslem rulers expelled from Spain all Jews who would not convert to Islam. Some Jewish physicians moved to other, still tolerant parts of the Moslem world. For example, Moses ben Maimon, better known as Maimonides, was born and trained as a physician in Córdoba; forced to leave Spain, he moved to Cairo, where he became personal physician to the Moslem leader Saladin. However, many Jewish medical practitioners moved north, spreading throughout Europe, where they nourished the new medical training centers of Europe.

Pilgrims to the Near East, especially Crusaders in the 11th to 14th centuries, also brought European Christians in touch with the learning of the Moslem world. European physicians traveling with Christian armies came into contact with new techniques and brought copies of some manuscripts back to Europe with them. Religious orders, such as the Knights of St. John Hospitalers, who established hospitals throughout the Mediterranean for the recuperation of wounded soldiers and pilgrims visiting the Holy Land, also passed Moslem medical knowledge on to Europe.

In these same centuries, Christian Europe was becoming more open to accepting new medical knowledge. The Christian Church had relaxed its earlier disapproval of the practice of medicine, so much so in fact that medicine was now practiced primarily in monasteries and abbeys. Originally founded by charitable religious groups, these institutions gradually extended their view of what was proper assistance to the poor and sick. Hospices, which had once merely provided shelter, gradually became hospitals that provided medical care. As a result, many *monks* and *nuns* became nurses and physicians; they were eager to find new ways to provide better medical care, and they drew partly on records from the past. Monasteries attracted some of the most talented people in Europe. Only there could medieval students learn Latin, the scholarly language for many centuries to come, and thereby have access to the learning of the world. Unfortunately, though, monastic physicians, being cut off from the practical tradition of medicine, had an excessive regard for the written works of the past; they also had a need to fit new knowledge into a restrictive religious view. As a result, the works that spread to Europe, and those that circulated from the monastic libraries—especially the works of Galen, Avicenna, Rhazes, and Hippocrates—were given Christian interpretations and then regarded as sacred texts, not to be questioned. Although this attitude was undercut by new learning in some areas, it persisted surprisingly long in others. As late as 1559, the College of Physicians in London demanded that one of its members retract a statement that Galen's work contained errors—and he did so.

Only a very elementary medicine was practiced outside the monasteries and abbeys. Some physicians had received their training in monasteries, which were far less cloistered and restrictive in those early centuries than they would be later; people could choose to leave them and work in the world. Monastery-trained physicians were often attached to the royal court, serving the nobility. But outside the monastery tradition there still existed wandering physicians. Some specialized in a particular type of operation, passing their secret skill from generation to generation within a family. Some were simply barber-surgeons, who performed most surgery in the medieval period, for monks and nuns did not wish to do such "manual work." Others worked as more general medical practitioners; these were the heirs to the remnants of classical medical traditions that were carried on as folk healing.

In areas without monasteries, medical practice was often centered in the physician's home; seriously ill patients sometimes stayed there during treatment, a practice that continued for centuries in rural and frontier parts of the world. Early Irish physicians were, indeed, obliged to leave their doors open for patients at all times. Because physicians always had to be available for emergency aid, they called on a variety of other people as assistants, to help them provide round-the-clock coverage. Apprentices (who were paying to learn the art), barbers, and apothecaries were often employed as assistants; in addition, many physicians trained members of their families to help them, not only sons, but also daughters, wives, and sisters. Rudimentary though it may have been, this provided the first systematic medical training open to women.

The first organized revival of medicine in Christian Europe was centered in Salerno, near Naples, in southern

Italy. A health spa and Greek settlement even before the emergence of the Roman Empire, Salerno had in medieval times become a refuge, first from the Goths who took Rome and later from Moslems. That the city was near the monastery library of Monte Cassino made it a natural place for a medical school to emerge. Traditionally said to have been founded in the ninth century by four physicians—a Jew, a Greek, a Latin, and an Arab—the secular medical school at Salerno was unique in being open to all nationalities and religions as well as to both sexes. In the 11th century it was enriched by Constantine of Africa, who brought to it a collection of medical manuscripts gathered in his travels through the Near East. In the 12th century it followed the Islamic lead by introducing medical licensing, and it revived Hippocratic ideas of medical ethics.

By the 13th century, all students at Salerno were required to study logic for three years and medicine and surgery for five years; to practice under a master physician for at least one year; and to pass a public examination by master physicians before being licensed to practice. Salernitan medicine became famous and the school drew students, including monks, from throughout Europe. Contributing to Salerno's fame was the popularity of a medical textbook, *Regimen Sanitatis Salernitanum,* a work of medical advice in rhymed couplets (for ease of memorization), which went through hundreds of editions and was used by some physicians even into the 17th century.

By the 13th century, other secular universities began to eclipse Salerno. The most important of those offering medical training were in Montpellier (a school that may have been founded as early as the eighth or ninth century by Spanish Jews who had left Islamic Spain for southern France) and in Bologna, Padua, and Naples in Italy. All of these universities drew teachers and students from both the Christian and Islamic worlds. Freed from religious restrictions, the faculty in these schools began to perform public anatomical dissections, the first since

Alexandria. Initially these dissections added little to knowledge of anatomy, since the actual dissection was usually performed by a barber-surgeon, while the physician stood on a platform describing, from copies of old manuscripts, the anatomical parts supposedly exposed. (If the text and reality disagreed, the text was assumed to be correct.) The first physician to do his own dissection was Mondino de Luzzi of Bologna, in the early 1300s; he was often assisted by his female student, Alexandra Galiani, who prepared the body. This pattern was not followed elsewhere, however, and anatomical dissection generally remained in the hands of uneducated barber-surgeons for two centuries more.

Unfortunately, while interest in anatomy and surgery was reviving in Italy and southern France, new universities in northern Europe, especially in Paris, Oxford, Prague, and Vienna, were pursuing a different course. There the universities, although supposedly secular, were very much under the domination of the Christian church. Members of religious orders, still virtually the only educated people in the area, formed most of the faculty. Many were under vows of celibacy, and in some places the tie with monasteries was so close that both faculty and students bore the shaved head, or tonsure, of monks. (Women were barred from northern universities, as they were later from southern ones.) Church influence on northern universities had strong adverse effects on medical training. In an effort to focus the attention of priests and monks more firmly on religion, the church in the 12th century forbade the clergy to practice medicine. When that edict was widely ignored, the command was modified to apply only to surgery. Although the practical effects of this ban were limited, surgery being mostly performed by barber-surgeons, the main point was made: in the church's eyes, medicine was a lesser art; theology was considered the highest study. In some colleges, the study of medicine was even forbidden, and in others only a few students were allowed to study medicine each year. Surgery was

In this classroom from the medical school at 15th-century Bologna, the headdresses indicate the varied ethnic backgrounds of the students. (Biblioteca Angelica, Rome, Ms. 596, fol. 1)

excluded from these universities altogether, making formal a split between medicine and surgery that had existed in northern Europe for several centuries.

As a result, medicine in northern Europe became a subject bound to book-learning, part of a liberal arts curriculum, with no practical experience offered or required. For example, before the mid-14th century, Paris medical students needed no practical apprenticeship before being granted a degree of bachelor or master of medicine; after that, they had to practice two summers outside Paris or one summer within Paris under a master. Nor was this experience very practical, for physicians during this period were mainly consultants; "hands-on" physical examinations were frowned upon. Physicians primarily gave consultations, often in groups, sometimes even publishing their opinions.

The field of university-trained physicians was even

further constricted in northern Europe as the course of study lengthened for those who wished to earn the title *"doctor."* That title, coming into use for the first time, was required of all who would teach at the university level. Oxford, for example, required 13 to 15 years of study in order to become a doctor of medicine, after which the doctor had to remain at Oxford another two years as a lecturer. In some northern universities the doctor was also required to take priestly orders and to maintain a celibate life. With such a lengthy course of study, and with restrictions on entering and practicing medicine, there existed for centuries a chronic shortage of university-trained physicians, both to practice and to teach.

Not surprisingly, these doctors of medicine were largely ineffective. Their university medicine, divorced from the practical trial and error that might enlighten and inform, increasingly relied on the scientific dead ends perpetuated by Islamic physicians, especially astrology and uroscopy. These late medieval physicians of northern Europe carried with them series of tables containing information about the moon and planets, rules for bleeding patients (some places required physicians to follow these rules exactly), and descriptions and interpretations of urine samples. Indeed the symbols of the medieval physician were these tables, which hung in strips from a belt around his waist, and the flask of urine, which he was almost always pictured as examining. Because uroscopy required analysis only of the urine, the physician might never even see the patient, who would simply send a flask of urine (in a special carrier built for the purpose) by messenger to him. Physicians responded with advice that was as cautious and often as generally and widely applicable as modern horoscopes.

Since university-trained physicians were scarce, expensive, and often ineffective, a whole range of other medical practitioners developed further in these centuries. Following the Islamic pattern, a separate class of apothecaries developed in Europe. In many places, they were by law evenly spaced around the country to place drugs in reach of any who needed them. Although trained in Latin, these apothecaries had much less schooling than physicians, often only apprenticeship. Being both cheaper and more accessible than university-trained physicians, apothecaries generally operated as general practitioners or junior physicians, especially in the countryside. Physicians and apothecaries often worked closely together. Sometimes they were united in the same guild, in less populated areas even being combined with *greengrocers* (because they sold herbs) and *artists* (because they used vegetable and animal pigments). Physicians were responsible for supervising apothecaries and their work, except where separate apothecary guilds took over the policing of their own members. Physicians occasionally used apothecary shops as consulting rooms; they were frequently partners in apothecary shops, sharing the profits, except where regulations forbade such partnerships.

Also serving the general public were a group of medical practitioners who had no university training but only apprenticeship with other non-degree physicians. Because they learned by practice and observation, they came to be called *"empirics,"* a term used to distinguish them from the book-trained physicians. Although in later centuries they became known as charlatans, in these early centuries empirics were sometimes more effective healers than academic physicians. They at least had the advantage of not being bound by Latin texts, so many could and did learn from practical experience with patients, and they passed their learning on to their apprentices. A significant number of them were women, who were barred both from university training and from the medical training that in earlier times they could have received in religious orders or in the earliest medical schools. Some were midwives, who had treated female ailments for many centuries; others had some training in pharmacy.

Unfortunately, because empirics were usually untrained in Latin, which was the medium of academic discourse, they were cut off from any new medical learning beyond the observation of their own immediate circle; any contributions they might have made to the advance of medical knowledge usually went no farther than their own apprentices.

If apothecaries and empirics were second-class citizens of medicine, surgeons were definitely third class. Not only was surgery seen as menial but surgeons were from the lower classes and were generally illiterate. Indeed, since surgery was so neglected a field, it did not really exist as a distinct occupation in the late Middle Ages. The early form of the term *"chirurgeon,"* which meant simply "a worker with the hands," was applied indiscriminately to anyone who had a sharp knife, a powerful arm, and a strong stomach. Under the direction of a physician, barber-surgeons carried out the little major surgery performed in these centuries; on their own, they also did minor surgery, performed bleeding, pulled teeth, and set fractures and dislocations. Wound surgeons, who accompanied military forces, specialized in treating battle injuries. However, a whole range of people—from a hog-gelder to an executioner—might also be called upon to do surgical work. In addition, there were still families of specialist surgeons, as well as many wandering surgeons claiming to have all skills, who performed as well as they could, took their money, and disappeared without waiting for the result (failure might cost them their lives).

University-trained physicians, as "pure advisers," were entitled to receive their consultation fee regardless of the outcome of the patient's illness. In contrast, other medical practitioners in the late Middle Ages generally worked for a fee specified by contract, often with part of the money paid before treatment began, the balance given when the cure was complete. Healers occasionally had to bring legal action to obtain fees owed them, but patients were not required to pay if the cure was not successful.

As the Christian church gradually succeeded in

The physicians of Salerno have their dinner, while the life of the wards goes on around them. (From Regimen Sanitatis Salernitatum, 1553, National Library of Medicine, Bethesda, Maryland)

forbidding the clergy to practice medicine, physicians worked under contract to religious orders. However, many religious orders ignored the official contract physician, defying papal ban by consulting Jewish physicians, who were generally trained in the highly regarded southern European universities. Gradually there developed independent hospitals that were not affiliated with monasteries and convents. Then physicians began to establish contractual connections with them, although nurses and priests still had the final say in all hospital matters, including medical questions.

The Rise of Surgery

Although the surgeons of the late Middle Ages were a motley group, it was from them that much of the revival of medicine would come during the Renaissance, following the upheavals of the late Middle Ages. The Black Death, the bubonic plague that struck Europe during the 14th century, came in the wake of the Crusades to the Near East and the widening of sea travel; in some parts of Europe, over one-third of the population died. Physicians, few and ineffective, often fled but many surgeons and apothecaries stayed behind and, as a result, these practitioners were accorded higher status by the general population. In addition, civil wars and papal schisms in Italy and southern France lessened the dominance of the southern medical schools. Gunpowder was also introduced in this period, important here because—like the plague—it created medical problems that could not be dealt with by reference to classical texts.

The way was open for medical innovation in northern Europe. Guy de Chauliac, a Frenchman who had studied medicine and theology at Montpellier and anatomy under Mondinus at Bologna, wrote a surgical text, *Chirurgia Magna,* in the 14th century. He also originated new, more effective methods of operating on bladder stones and cataracts, and of dealing with bone fractures. Anatomical dissections were done more frequently than the previous ratio—generally one body a year per medical school—had allowed. Physicians began to do their own dissections, not to demonstrate ancient learning but to learn new facts about anatomy and physiology, as well as to correct old misinformation. Such learning was unwelcome and dangerous in some circles. For example, Spanish surgeon Michael Servetus published a book detailing the circulation of blood through the lungs (75 years before William Harvey's discoveries about the circulatory system). For this he was hounded out of Paris and, on his way to Italy, was arrested in Geneva in 1553 and burned at the stake, along with his books, for heresy.

The finest anatomist of the time was Andreas Vesalius, a Belgian surgeon who studied in Paris. Like most anatomists of the time, he haunted gallows and graveyards, searching for fresh corpses to dissect—a practice not calculated to please the Christian church or to ease popular fear of dissectionists. Moving on to Italy, to teach at Bologna and Padua, Vesalius met artists who produced, under his direction, the extraordinary illustrations for *De Humani Corporis Fabrica,* (*On the Fabric of the Human Body*). This revolutionary work on anatomy laid the basis for future anatomical work.

With new, better understanding of anatomy, surgery once again began to develop. As Guy de Chauliac put it: "A surgeon who does not know his anatomy is like a blind man hewing a log." That described only too well centuries of surgery, in which the internal organs of the body had been unknown territory. Only in 16th-century Europe did surgeons begin to operate with anything that approached an understanding of anatomy. Anatomists, however, were primarily physicians who were broadening their knowledge of the human body. Those who sparked the development of modern surgery were uneducated barber-surgeons.

Foremost among them was Ambroise Paré, originally a barber, then a wound-dresser at the Paris Hôtel Dieu. Paré made surgical history while working as a military surgeon, where he dealt not only with conventional wounds but also with gunshot wounds. Traditional treatment of wounds and amputations involved the application of boiling oil or a cauterizing iron (following Islamic practice). But Paré discovered, on once running out of oil, that patients treated with oil fared far worse than those left alone. After that he ceased such applications. He also rediscovered and reintroduced many techniques that

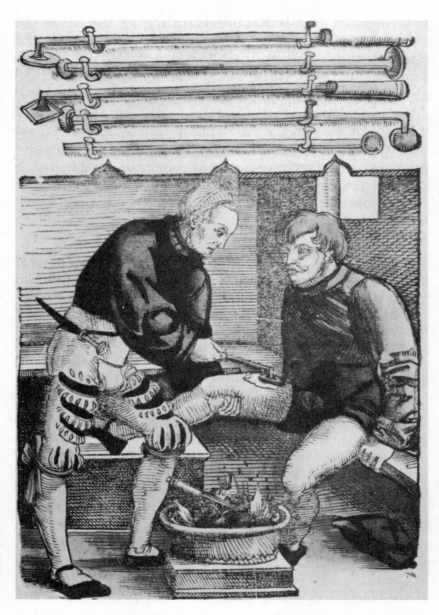

Using techniques developed by Moslem practitioners, this 16th-century barber-surgeon is cauterizing a patient's thigh wound, employing an iron drawn from his varied collection. (By Johannes Wechtlin, from Feldtbuch der Wundartzney, *reproduced from* Medicine and the Artist [Ars Medica] *by permission of the Philadelphia Museum of Art)*

had been known to Hippocrates and his followers but had been forgotten by later Europeans. Among these was ligature to prevent hemorrhaging. Widely celebrated by soldiers and citizens for his humane attention to the patient's plight, Paré rose to become surgeon to the royal family of France. In the process, he went far toward changing the relationship between physicians and surgeons, especially in France, the dominant nation in surgical innovation at the time.

University medical schools still conducted their education of students entirely in Latin, as did the one surgical school, the College of St. Come, in Paris. Barber-surgeons had therefore been barred from formal training, since few knew Latin. But Paré, as the royal surgeon, was too distinguished a surgeon to remain excluded. His admission to the College of St. Come spurred the use of the vernacular (everyday language) in learned communication, at the same time raising the status of the working surgeon. In this same period, surgeons who performed medical operations began to separate themselves from barbers who focused on grooming functions. The former were known in France as "surgeons of the long robe," their professional dress being long academic gowns; barbers were known as "surgeons of the short robe," since they wore short jerkins indicating their lower station in society.

Relations were also complicated between physicians and surgeons. Physicians preferred to keep surgeons as lowly assistants, and they protested against raising their status. In France some physicians even established lectures and training courses for barbers, using them as surgical assistants, instead of calling in trained surgeons. Near the turn of the 17th century, some surgical specialties emerged, splitting off from the general practice of surgery. Those who specialized in treating teeth began to be called *chirurgien-dentist (surgeon-dentist)*, which was later shortened to simply dentist. Surgeons also began to move into the childbirth process, at first calling themselves "man midwives" and later adopting the titles *accoucheur* (primarily in France) and *obstetrician*.

Distinctions between various practitioners had some importance among the rich in the great European cities;

but medical practice in rural areas and among the poor was little affected by such controversies or new discoveries. Most dispensers of medical advice continued to be empirics, barber-surgeons, apothecaries, apprentices or heirs in possession of some special medical secret, or other traveling practitioners. Sometimes they were simply educated people who carried with them a store of the standard drugs of the time.

Such was certainly the case in the new colonies to which Europeans spread in the 16th and 17th centuries. The earliest English colonies in North America had no trained physicians. While a few surgeons operated, most medical care was provided by clergymen, including Samuel Fuller, who arrived on the *Mayflower,* and Cotton Mather. Medical provisions were somewhat better in the Latin American colonies, where Spanish explorers had found cultures with sophisticated medications. Indeed, the first Spaniards arriving in Peru sent back word that no doctors need be sent, since Incan physicians had more effective cures. The Native Americans were soon ravaged by European diseases, however. In many areas their medical system was destroyed, remaining only in specific medications and folk cures. The Spanish soon set up their own systems, starting the first universities in the Americas, in Mexico and Peru in 1551, publishing the first medical text in 1570, and establishing the first chair of medicine, at the University of Mexico in 1580.

Influences from America contributed to the scientific explosion and the social upheaval of the 17th century. Returning explorers and pirate surgeons brought to Europe many new herbs and drugs from around the world. By demonstrating that the ancient pharmacopeias (books describing drugs) were not complete, they spurred research in the development of new medicines, notably by the Swiss researcher Paracelsus. Medicinal chemistry rose from the ashes of the dying alchemy. Travelers also brought back less welcome things, including new diseases that caused many new epidemics, especially of syphilis and plague. Physicians began to look more closely at diseases, distinguishing between diseases that had for centuries been thought to be one. New instruments such as the microscope, developed in the 17th century, assisted physicians in their fresh examination of diseases. Scientific societies and professional associations were founded, replacing the medieval trade guilds. And medical journals were established, the first in Paris in 1679, allowing physicians and surgeons to share their ideas and discoveries more readily.

New methods of medical education began to emerge in northern Europe, which was now largely Protestant. At the Leiden medical school in the Netherlands, founded in 1579, a team of medical educators led by Hermann Boerhaave, introduced the practice of clinical teaching, combining classroom work with study of patients in an affiliated hospital. Boerhaave also stressed comparison of diagnosis with the observed course of the disease and with results of autopsies, as Hippocratic physicians had recommended 2,000 years earlier. Students and faculty from all over Europe—Protestant, Catholic, and Jewish—who would have once gone to the major medical schools of southern Europe, now flocked to Leiden. They then spread out to establish other medical schools based on the same principles; the most important of these were the Medical School of Vienna (the Old Vienna School) and the Edinburgh Medical School. Their graduates further spread the ideas of clinical education.

In 1765, the first medical school in the North American colonies was founded at what is now the University of Pennsylvania in Philadelphia. Staffed by graduates of the Edinburgh school, it had among its faculty John Morgan, William Shippen, Jr., and Benjamin Rush. Apprenticeship training was still common, however, and could be very effective. For example, the first black physician in the United States, James Derham, learned medical practice as a slave to two physicians; later he earned his freedom and in 1790 began practicing medicine in New Orleans. Benjamin Rush, with whom he studied as a free man, said of Derham: "I thought I could

Far from wearing protective clothing, this 17th-century barber-surgeon is dressed in high style for bleeding his fashionable patient. (By Abraham Bosse, Bibliothèque Nationale, Paris, Ed 30 rés., fol.)

give him information concerning the treatment of diseases, but I learned more from him than he could expect from me."

Hand in hand with the establishment of clinical teaching was the anatomical work of the 17th and 18th centuries. Such great anatomists as William Harvey, the English physician who detailed the circulation of blood, and John Hunter, the Scottish physician whose wide-ranging study of anatomy and physiology helped develop modern surgery, led the way. Like Vesalius, under whom Harvey's teacher had studied at Padua, most anatomists were short of corpses for their work. They sometimes ran into legal difficulties for bribing the *dead-house keepers* for bodies. They also created a specialized group of graverobbers called *resurrection men,* who provided bodies for a fee. Gradually, however, the laws were changed to provide sufficient corpses for anatomical education. In some places, such as Vienna, the pendulum swung the other way and virtually all who died in hospitals were dissected by students or resident physicians.

While these northern European physicians were exploring new medical frontiers, most medical education and practice still followed the old ways. Classical texts, although purged during the Renaissance of many errors introduced by medieval transcriptions, continued to dominate medical diagnosis and treatment. The most common treatments were clysters (enemas), bleeding, and purges, all of which continued to be used through the 18th century and well into the 19th. Indeed, in the early 19th century, French physicians revived the practice of bleeding (sometimes called "therapeutic vampirism") to such an extent that over 41 million leeches a year were used in France alone. Among the many who seem to have been, in effect, bled to death by ignorant doctors were George Washington and the poet Lord Byron. The incompetence of many physicians and the ineffectiveness of old-fashioned medicine made medical doctors objects of ridicule in the popular arts of the time.

Reunion of Physicians and Surgeons

As a result, the 18th and 19th centuries saw continuing realignments among various groups of medical practitioners, each struggling to enlarge and consolidate its domain. The first change was the gradual reunion of physicians and surgeons into one discipline. These two groups had been treated as virtual coequals in Italy since the Renaissance. They were combined into one category in the Scottish schools and therefore in the Scottish-influenced American schools as well. France, although it was the home of modern surgery, was somewhat slower in bringing about the full equality of surgeons. In England the change came very slowly, not before late in the 19th century. Until then, physicians and surgeons divided up medical practices in often absurd ways, to the point where some English physicians, as late as the 1860s, seriously discussed whether administration of drugs by means of a needle was a violation of "pure" medicine and an incursion into the surgeon's area.

Whatever their official relationships, physicians and surgeons were becoming socially indistinguishable. Except for slight variations in academic dress worn on formal occasions, they dressed the same. During the 18th century, this was usually in fashionable clothes, aristocratic physicians and successful quacks being most richly dressed. Physicians and surgeons generally carried a sword (still the mark of a gentleman); wore spurs for riding to patients; and sported the special doctor's wig, called a "physical" wig. In the 19th century, wigs went out of fashion, and the doctor's costume became the more spare, formal black suit, cut in the latest style, often accompanied by a gold or silver-headed cane. The doctor's bag, containing medicines and tools, completed the picture.

Over the years physicians also faced continuing challenges to their status, authority, and responsibility from pharmacists and nurses. (See separate articles on these occupations.) At the beginning of the 18th century, medical licensing was widely variable, and medical practitioners existed at many levels. The top level was achieved only by physicians who had received doctorates from prestigious schools, which were usually restricted to people from the upper classes; in England, for example, only graduates of Oxford, Cambridge, or Trinity College in Dublin could be members of the Royal College of Physicians.

The middle level, sometimes called the licentiate, was for physicians (mostly from the middle classes) who had attended other schools. In some countries, the licentiate's privileges were somewhat restricted compared to the full doctor's; this was true though his education might have been as good as or even better than the full doctor's if he had gone to a school like Edinburgh or Leiden.

The lower level consisted of people with less education, who generally operated as doctors to the poor, especially in rural areas. Usually people from the middle classes,

Gulliver's Travels

This pompous, bewigged 18th-century physician carries both a fancy cane and a sword as signs of his exalted station. (From Gulliver's Travels)

they had often worked as apothecaries or country surgeons for a few years in order to earn money to continue their schooling and move to a higher level. Such practitioners supplied medical care to most of the country. In England, these practitioners were so well-regarded by the public that physicians lost the battle to keep apothecaries from practicing medicine; in the late 19th century apothecaries merged into the medical profession along with surgeons. (*Druggists* and *pharmaceutical chemists* emerged to simply supply medicines.) Such a merging did not occur in the rest of Europe, where the apothecary remained distinct from the physician, although of equal status.

In continental Europe, the bachelor of medicine operated as a lower-level medical practitioner, until uniform educational requirements were established for all physicians and surgeons. As always, an underclass of untrained, unlicensed healers and street doctors continued to practice, hawking products ranging from "cough syrup" laced with laudanum to "mummy powder," supposedly imported directly from Egypt, and running "medicine shows" to help sell their products in city and country. But gradually unlicensed physicians and surgeons passed out of the picture as license restrictions became general in Europe.

Another group with whom physicians had to settle relations was nurses. Since the adoption of Christianity by Rome in the fourth century, hospitals (at first more like nursing homes) had been under the direction of nurses, under church control in the beginning, then often under municipal or state control. Physicians and surgeons were attached to hospitals by contract for consultation only, having no official or administrative standing. Doctors who worked with the military nursing orders during the Crusades were treated with honor—nurses and junior officers stood when they entered the room—but that was exceptional; it grew out of the religious orders' high regard for military form. More typically, the physician was disregarded or obliged to fit into the hospital routine established by the head nurse, who wielded a great deal of power. For example, in the 17th century, when St. Vincent de Paul founded the Sisters of Charity nursing order, he found it necessary to instruct the nurses to obey physicians' instructions and to treat them with respect. At the turn of the 18th century, a head nurse in the Hôtel Dieu in Paris was still insisting that physicians should make hospital rounds only at the times that had been specified by the nursing staff some decades earlier; she also complained that doctors did not treat nurses with the same deference as in the past, indicating the shift of the balance between the two groups. While nurses in Catholic hospitals were often well-disciplined and highly motivated, nurses in Protestant countries in those pre-Florence Nightingale days were not. Physicians and surgeons in Protestant areas therefore were more respected and had greater authority, especially in medical matters, although head nurses still ran the hospitals.

Physicians and nurses had conflicts in other areas as well. In Protestant countries, military medicine was entirely in the hands of physicians; British surgeons initially even refused the help of Florence Nightingale's nursing brigade, so jealous were they of their territory. (Armies from Catholic countries were generally tended by nursing orders.) Nor did physicians uniformly welcome the arrival of trained nurses, many fearing that they would take over some of their medical duties and privileges. Students and junior doctors, who often made extra money tending patients in their homes, were unhappy to be replaced by trained nurses, many of whom moved into private duty. Indeed, in the United States, these nurses had little choice; relatively few trained nurses were employed in hospitals, the doctors preferring to have their hospitals staffed by untrained young women. In a peculiar development, many doctors established small private hospitals with "nursing schools" connected; that allowed them to have unpaid nurses working long hours during their course of study, which anyway involved much apprenticeship. Once graduated, however, few trained nurses were employed in these, or any, hospitals; they were forced into private duty. Even Dr. Charles Mayo, of the famous Mayo Clinic in Rochester, Minnesota, preferred to use untrained "country girls" as nurses. By the end of the 19th century, doctors had generally established their authority over nurses, nowhere more so than in the United States. In some places nurses were required to stand when a doctor entered the room and to open the door for him. Appreciation of the usefulness of a trained nurse's skills and establishment of a partnership between the two groups did not develop until medicine itself had changed.

Medicine in the 19th century was transformed by such scientific advances as the practice of vaccinations, developed by Edward Jenner. (Although the idea of inoculation had been imported from the East decades earlier, it had been perceived as too dangerous to use, and it had even been legally forbidden in parts of the United States.) Histology (the study of tissues), physiology, pathology, embryology, chemotherapy, and bacteriology all began modern development in the 19th century, placing the laboratory once and for all at the center of medical work. Many techniques associated today with routine medical examinations were put into practice at this time. The 18th century had seen doctors begin to time the pulse and use the newly developed clinical thermometer. The technique of percussion (tapping the chest for echoes to indicate lung ailments) was developed in the same period and popularized in the 19th century. Auscultation (listening to the sounds of the heart) had a history as far back as Hippocrates; but the stethoscope was developed only in the 19th century, when a French physician used a tube of paper to magnify the heart sounds of a patient. With the development of such practical examination techniques, medicine moved from a "pure" theoretical discipline toward becoming a "hands-on" profession.

Practical discoveries also laid the necessary basis for modern surgery. The main hazards involved in surgery had always been pain (and the resulting medical condition of shock), infection, and hemorrhage. The rediscovery of ligature by Paré allowed surgeons to control hemorrhage to a large extent. However, such knowledge was double-edged, because ligature also permitted surgeons to remove major limbs, which previously they had avoided doing except when absolutely necessary. Some surgeons now even began to specialize in these operations. Pain made speed vital, so before the introduction of modern pain relievers, slow, careful surgical repair was impossible.

The first of the anesthetic gases was isolated in England in the late 18th century; in the 19th century such gases were used at popular "sniffing parties" and music hall shows. They were not applied to medicine, however, until the 1840s, with various American surgeons credited with being the first to do so. Anesthetic gases not only prevented excruciating pain but also kept the patient from going into shock. Unfortunately, some surgeons of the time thought that shock, which causes the circulatory system to slow dramatically, was necessary to patients during operations, in order to slow the flow of blood. They therefore refused to use anesthetics, especially on soldiers, who were believed to be still in a state of "battle tension" and not in need of pain relievers. Within decades, however, anesthetics became widely accepted, allowing surgery to pass from a profession of speed and brawn to one of delicacy and high skill.

The problem of infection still existed and had, since medieval times, even been seen as a virtue by many surgeons. Through a misunderstanding of Hippocratic writings, Galen had written of "laudable pus." In the Dark Ages, when Galen's word was gospel, surgeons placed ointments and dressings on patients' wounds in deliberate attempts to produce pus. Antisepsis (killing germs to prevent infection) sometimes occurred accidentally, as when wine or similar solutions were used to

With the smoke of battle in the background, these Civil War surgeons are tending to the wounded, some being carried in and others brought by horse ambulance. The young man in the center is carrying on his back a portable medicine chest. (By Winslow Homer, National Library of Medicine, Bethesda, Maryland)

cleanse wounds, or when burning oil or cautery was used to stop bleeding and seal the wound. In addition, linen used in battle dressings was often reused to save money and was partly disinfected by washing and ironing. But physicians knew nothing about germs until later.

Accidental antisepsis virtually disappeared in the 19th-century teaching hospitals, however, There corpses (none of them embalmed or disinfected) were now provided in abundance for dissections. This made conditions far worse for patients. Doctors wore no special uniforms in those days, not even to protect their clothes, although some doctors wore old, soiled suit coats while actually performing operations. Nor did the doctors or any of the staff wash themselves or their tools before working on a patient—even if they had just come from dissecting a corpse. Operations were often social events of a sort, carried out in public rooms before outside visitors as well as students. It is not surprising that the surgical mortality rate ran as high as 80 percent.

By the beginning of the 19th century, some doctors were urging that the medical staff wash themselves and their surrounding before operations; other doctors protested indignantly at the idea that a "gentleman's hands" could carry disease. Not until the 1860s did Joseph Lister (the first physician to be made an English lord) propose the practice of destroying germs, the existence of which had been discovered only a few years before by Louis Pasteur. This was done at first by spraying or dripping carbolic acid on the wound area; the medical staff still took no special precautions with themselves, their tools, or their surroundings. But toward the end of the century, as Lister's ideas spread to other countries, his work evolved into a theory promoting "asepsis," the exclusion of germs from the operating area. Operating gowns began to be used; sterilization of instruments by steam was introduced by a German physician, Ernst von Bergmann. In the early 20th century an American surgeon, William Stewart Halsted, introduced the use of rubber gloves, initially to protect the hands of a surgical nurse (later his wife) who was allergic to the disinfectant used in "scrubbing up." Some surgical staff members quickly recognized the value of wearing gloves that could be sterilized; others refused to wear them until thinner gloves were available. In Europe, some surgeons wore sterilized cloth gloves over their rubber gloves for extra protection. Exclusion of improperly garbed outsiders did not come about until the 20th century, and surgical masks were not widely used until after World War II. Each step toward asepsis created correspondingly better conditions for the rapid progress in surgical procedures achieved in the 20th century.

With the increasing importance of practical techniques, medicine shifted from a relatively passive, consultative role to a more active one characterized by doctors' greater willingness and ability to intervene with new medicines and surgery. As medicine grew more sophisticated, the traditional hospitals changed from shelters for the poor and dying to places for diagnosis, treatment, operation, and recovery. The small private doctors' hospitals that had proliferated in the 19th century gave way to large modern centers of medical care. The relationship between doctors and nurses also evolved into its modern form. Nurses continued to carry out much of the day-to-day administration of the hospital, with the head nurse retaining a good deal of power (especially in European hospitals), but the hospital came to be under the overall control of physicians and professional administrators. Nurses lost power in the exchange but they gained respect for their developing skills. As medicine became increasingly complex, nurses along with other allied health practitioners took over functions formerly performed by doctors, leaving doctors free to do work demanding greater skills. This constant shift has sparked continual legal redefinitions of various medical practitioners' functions; official approval has often followed actual practice by some decades.

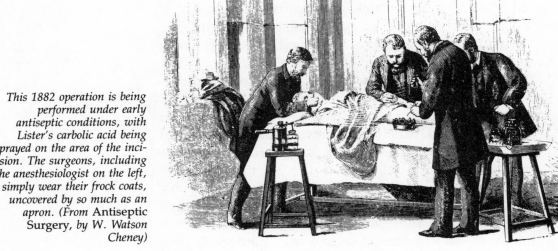

Modern Medical Education

In the 19th century more standardized educational
requirements for and registration or licensing of practicing physicians and surgeons were established, in part because of the larger role professional medicine played in
people's lives; but modern criteria still vary widely. In
general, medical study consists of at least five or six years
of university study, followed by a year or two of internship
in a hospital. In south, east, and central Europe, medical
education tends to emphasize formal lectures,
accompanied by practical demonstrations. Elsewhere in
Europe and in America, medical education takes a more
clinical approach, with practical hospital experience starting earlier in the course of medical studies. In most
European countries, prospective physicians are required
to pass public examinations, set by medical schools under
the supervision of the national government.

Education and licensing in Great Britain and the
British Commonwealth followed different patterns than

in other countries. The Medical Act of 1858 created the General Medical Council, composed almost entirely of physicians, to supervise medical education and maintain a register of qualified physicians and surgeons. When "pure" medicine and surgery were still divided, the degrees awarded were either bachelor of medicine (M.B.) or bachelor of surgery (B.S. or Ch.B, if the old spelling of chirurgery had been retained). Only those who completed a further course of study received a doctor of medicine (M.D.) degree and were entitled to be called "doctor"; holders of the bachelor's degree were properly called "mister." For surgeons, "mister" was a term of pride and distinction; even after physicians and surgeons became united in modern medicine, many English surgeons—including those with M.D. degrees—preferred to be called "mister."

The United States is another special case in medical education and licensing. In the 19th century, although some well-trained European doctors had emigrated to practice in America, most practitioners still had only a minimum of education, primarily apprenticeships. A wide open frontier and a rapidly increasing population created such a need for new doctors that few questions were asked. Even at the "best" schools, medical courses generally consisted of 8 to 14 weeks of lectures, along with a one- or two-year apprenticeship. Calls for better medical education found few supporters. In 1847, when the newly formed American Medical Association recommended that the school year be extended to six months, the two schools that did so—the University of Pennsylvania and the College of Physicians and Surgeons in New York—quickly lost most of their students. In the 1870s, Harvard lengthened its medical program to three years and lost 40 percent of its students; despite this loss it and other schools stuck to the longer course. (In light of this it is not surprising that some American doctors feared competition from nurses; by the late 19th century, nurses generally had a three-year course of lectures and hospital practice.) Not until 1893 was the modern pattern of medical training established in the United States, at Johns Hopkins University; a college degree was mandatory for admission (unlike European medical schools), and the four-year course included not only lectures but extensive work in laboratories and the affiliated hospital.

National licensing also encouraged more uniform medical practice during this period. The power to license medical practitioners is vested in the individual states, which originally had widely varying standards; physicians who wished to operate in other states had to obtain approval from each state's licensing board. In 1915, a National Board of Medical Examiners was formed to provide an additional set of licensing examinations, open only to graduates of accredited medical schools. Since most states accept the results, a physician who passes these "boards" can practice almost anywhere in the United States.

In the 20th century, countries colonized by Europeans have generally adopted systems of licensing and education that combine the British and American ones. Most countries, especially in the British Commonwealth, adopted medical registers kept by general medical councils; Canada and some other countries also instituted national medical examination boards. The British Commonwealth countries generally award degrees that follow the British classifications. Many Third World countries award an M.D. degree after four to six years of study. The pattern of medical education set by Johns Hopkins has been influential throughout the world. Students from Asia and Africa have often gone to Europe or the United States for their medical training, sometimes staying to practice in their adopted land and sometimes returning to spread Western medical practices in their homelands. In many countries, however, these modern systems overlay traditional medical practices from before Colonial times; this creates a two-tier medical system, such as is prevalent in China.

While in the United States and Western European

countries medical occupations are distinct (with doctors' and nurses' training quite separate, for example), in the Soviet Union medical occupations follow a career path. A person's position within the medical hierarchy depends on the level reached in medical education; one may start as an orderly or nurse and progress to become a general physician or a specialist. Indeed, the Russians allow a lesser-grade physician to practice medicine. Called a *feldsher,* this practitioner is intermediate in training and responsibility between nurse and physician. The feldsher's existence continues an old pattern that exists all over the world wherever physicians and surgeons are rare. Even where physicians and surgeons are available, such people—variously called *nurse practitioners, physician's assistants,* or *surgeon's assistants*—increasingly carry out relatively routine medical duties in the absence of a physician, who performs only the most highly skilled work.

In the 19th and 20th centuries, bars against women and minority groups began to be dropped. Sparked by Elizabeth Blackwell, who received her medical degree from Geneva Medical College in New York State (the only school that would take her) in 1849, women in North American and Europe slowly began to move into medicine. They sometimes did so by founding all-women medical schools; Blackwell herself taught at all-women schools in New York and in her native England. Those women who completed training found that their difficulties were not over, however, for discrimination against them persisted when they were in practice. Indeed, a significant number of early women physicians actually worked as nurses, because they were better accepted in that role. At least one surgeon, Mary Walker, who operated during the American Civil War, dressed as a man.

Attitudes unfortunately change slowly. Even in the late 20th century, when many more women have obtained medical training, a smaller proportion of female physicians than of male actually practice their profession

Many women doctors, perhaps partly because they faced discrimination in private practice, entered public health fields. This doctor is examining immigrants at Ellis Island, New York, in the early 20th century. (Courtesy of American Museum of Immigration, Statue of Liberty, National Park Service, U.S. Department of the Interior)

in some countries, notably the United States. The Soviet Union is one of the few places where women have achieved anything like equality in medicine; since the medical education system there places no bars to progression within the medical hierarchy, women physicians actually outnumber men; men, however, still continue to hold the key decision-making roles in the government-controlled system.

Minority groups have also made progress in the 20th century, thanks to the efforts of world-wide equal rights movements. In the United States, for example, blacks were generally barred from medical schools, even after the Civil War, particularly in the South. In some areas, they had to set up their own medical schools. Only in the 20th century, under the pressure of civil rights movements beginning in the 1920s and most actively in the 1960s, did the barriers of segregation begin to break down. Oddly enough, the reversal of discrimination was so successful in some places that it resulted in a major court case charging medical schools with reverse discrimination favoring black applicants.

The Age of Specialization

In the 20th century, the most prominent feature of medical practice has been the trend towards specialization, especially in surgery. This trend, started in the 19th-century schools of Paris and Vienna (the New School), was made possible in its modern form by development of new technology including the X-ray at the turn of the century, blood transfusions (after blood types were distinguished), controlled respiration techniques, intravenous therapy, antibiotics and other new drugs, and—most recently—new tools such as laser beams and ultrasound. Training for medical specialties extends far beyond that required for the basic medical license; certification is generally handled by professional groups within that specialty.

One long-standing medical specialty is *ophthalmology,* the treatment of eye disorders. Most surgical and internal specialties could not develop in modern form until the technical advances of the past century. Plastic surgery techniques go back as far as early India, where surgeons replaced amputated noses, ears, and lips with flaps of skin taken from elsewhere on the patient's body. Considered a subclass of potters because of their working method, these early surgeons (and their medieval successors) were by any standards rough workers compared with today's *plastic surgeons* who perform delicate, complex reconstructive and cosmetic surgery. Likewise, the *neurologists* and *neurosurgeons* of today have only a passing resemblance to the ancient trepanners, who had virtually no knowledge of the workings and interconnections of the brain, spine, and the rest of the nervous system.

Some modern medical specialties, of course, had almost no historical counterparts. The *cardiologist* could not have arisen before the physiological importance of the heart was fully understood; that is, not before William Harvey's work in the 17th century. The specialty of the *internist,* who focuses on diseases of the internal organs, would have little cause to develop when the soft organs of the body were still unexplored. Nor would a subspecialty such as that of the *gastroenterologist,* who specializes in problems of the digestive system, have been possible. The specialties of *allergist* and *immunologist* are of very recent vintage as well, dependent as they are on modern testing techniques to identify defects, or allergical or immunological problems. The *dermatologist's* emergence as an important specialty may have been hindered by the view that skin was the province of the barber or beautician.

Other specialties are totally dependent on new technology. The *anesthesiologist* could emerge only after the discovery of the first of the anesthetic gases in the mid-19th century. In the rough-and-ready days of surgery, anesthetics were often given by medical students, later by nurse-anesthetists. Nurses still administer some relatively routine anesthetics, but modern surgical techniques, including operations that may last for 24 hours or more, require the skill provided by a physician with special training as an anesthesiologist.

The modern specialty of *radiologist* grew in the same way. After the discovery of radioactive substances and the X-ray machine, general practitioners and technicians sometimes operated such equipment, but the modern proliferation of scanning machines and radioactive treatments require the advanced training of a physician trained as a specialist.

Not all physicians work directly with patients. Many in the modern period have, for example, chosen to work in research and analysis, focusing on epidemiology, that is, isolating causes of diseases. Other specialists focus more sharply on individual cases, as does the *pathologist*. Some pathologists act, essentially, as consultants to other physicians, giving expert opinions on the extent of a particular disease. Pathologist are also often brought in to perform autopsies, to determine the cause of death, and to analyze the effects of a disease and its treatment. A highly visible subspecialty is that of *forensic pathology*. The forensic pathologist, who is called in to determine the cause of death, assessing whether it is a natural one, is an important member of the criminal investigation team.

Other physicians have developed specialties defined by the type of patient served. For example, specialists in *pediatrics* treat children, those in *geriatrics* treat the elderly, and those in *family medicine* treat the family as a whole, because the unit often has interconnected problems. Other doctors specialize in *travel medicine*, focusing on the special strains of unusual diseases that the traveler may be exposed to. A wider area is that of *industrial medicine*, which specializes in treating the hazards linked with modern industrial production. *Sports medicine* is a specialty that focuses on the problems of professional and amateur athletes. Doctors in sports and industrial medicine are often employed by people other than the patient; this may produce divided allegiances that break down the traditional confidentiality between doctors and patients.

Public health medicine has also become a major specialty of the 20th century. Many physicians chose to focus on the medical problems of less developed parts of the world where little medical care exists. At first working in conjunction with missionary movements, and more recently with United Nations organizations, physicians

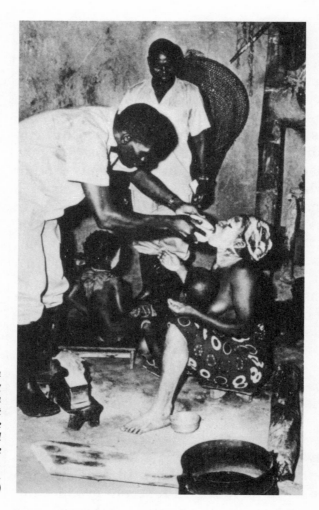

In many parts of the modern world, traditional healing methods coexist with modern scientific treatment. This West African woman has put white on her face to repulse evil spirits, while she takes medicine from a public health team. (World Health Organization, Geneva)

have been attempting to improve medical care in such areas. Rather than caring only for the affluent, such physicians are dedicated to raising the general level of a whole population's medical care. They often train local assistants for this purpose, in areas where the doctor-patient ratio may be one to many tens of thousands. In line with social reform movements, such procedures have been followed in poor, remote and inner-city areas of developed countries as well, in efforts to equalize available medical care.

Medical and non-medical specialists compete in certain areas, especially in the treatment of skeletal and muscular problems. *Orthopedists* are physicians who specialize in prevention and correction of such problems; physicians specializing in *physical medicine,* who are often called *physiatrists,* focus on rehabilitative therapy, using massage, hydrotherapy, and mechanical manipulation to the same end, often with the assistance of licensed *physical therapists.* Some of these treatments have been known from the beginning of human history, so other types of healers have not been inclined to let medical doctors monopolize their use. In some cases, alternate medical systems have developed. That is the case with osteopathic medicine, which is based on the idea that the body is a perfect machine. *Osteopathic physicians,* who began practicing in the mid-19th century United States, developed their own medical schools, hospitals, and practices, quite separate from main line (what they call allopathic) physicians. Originally they focused on hand manipulation of muscle and bone, but they have lately increased their use of drugs and surgery; in these changes as well as their tendency toward specialization they have increasingly come to resemble their medical colleagues.

Another alternative system of treatment is that of chiropractic, developed around the turn of the 20th century in the United States. In contrast to osteopathic physicians, *chiropractors* cannot use drugs or surgery; they focus entirely on manipulating the body, sometimes using diagnostic machines to aid them. Other practitioners also exist, as they have throughout history, who claim to have secret techniques to ease the world's ailments.

Despite the undoubted charlatanry of some non-standard healing practices, medicine has been accused of too readily throwing out traditional or folk medicine without examining it for any valuable residue. Such a potentially wasteful scientific attitude has been partly corrected in the 20th century, with physicians exploring medicines and techniques that have not been part of standard Western medicine. This exploration has been especially active in the area of Chinese medicine, which had been virtually ignored by Western physicians until recent decades. Some practitioners in traditional techniques, like *acupuncturists,* have gained qualified acceptance as specialists in Western countries. The difficult question for physicians and patients alike is how to evaluate such practitioners. Medical guilds and societies were supposedly established to protect the public from unscrupulous and ill-trained practitioners. But critics of restrictive licensing charge that physicians use it primarily to maintain their monopoly against healers who do not fit into standard medical niches. They also note that physicians are extremely slow to clear their own ranks of incompetent physicians. The boundaries between legal and illegal healers continues to shift, being defined by particular governments and, in modern times, often by health-insurance organizations, which have to settle the knotty questions of who is and who is not entitled to insurance payment for medical services.

Medicine in the 19th and 20th centuries also became more private. While early Greek and Indian medical oaths stressed privacy between physician and patient, medicine in the intervening centuries had remained a rather public affair. Only in recent centuries have physicians and surgeons developed truly private offices and, even then, mostly in advanced countries. Elsewhere, older patterns remain; a physician often has a literally open door during office hours, with patients on line examined and advised in view of all others. In the developed countries, too, clinics for the poor have a more public aspect about them.

The many changes in medicine in recent centuries have brought about corresponding changes in the physician's situation. The development of new techniques and technologies has given some physicians—especially specialist surgeons—higher status than at any time since physicians were worshiped as gods in ancient times. But such techniques also made many physicians less in-

With the rise of specialists, and the increasing concentration of medical care in office and hospital, family doctors who attended patients in their homes have almost completely disappeared. (By John Vachon, Library of Congress, LC-USF34-64221-D)

dependent. The difficulty of keeping up with rapidly expanding medical knowledge and the cost of maintaining expensive equipment have caused many physicians to operate out of group practices; they are also closely tied to hospitals in which they perform most of their work. In addition, social reforms sparked by the increasing costs of medical care and by its inequitable distribution have caused many countries to institute national health-care systems. In such systems physicians and surgeons are paid salaries and are no longer medical entrepreneurs—independent business owners, in effect. Hierarchies develop in these massive health-care institutions, making many junior physicians and surgeons powerless underlings employed by an impersonal, seemingly uncontrollable organization; some physicians have even formed unions to attempt to regain power within these systems, a situation that would have been unthinkable even a century ago. As health care is one of the fastest-growing occupational areas in the world, these tendencies are likely to be intensified, further stratifying the work that was, not so long ago, performed by the lone physician.

For related occupations in this volume, *Healers,* see the following:

Barbers
Dentists
Midwives and Obstetricians
Nurses
Pharmacists
Psychologists and Psychiatrists
Veterinarians

For related occupations in other volumes of the series, see the following:
in *Scholars and Priests:*
Monks and Nuns
Priests
in *Scientists and Technologists:*
Alchemists
Biologists
Chemists
in *Warriors and Adventurers:*
Soldiers

Psychiatrists and Psychologists

Psychiatry and psychology are essentially modern occupations, arising as distinct specialties only in the 18th century. But both professions have their roots in ancient practices and beliefs related to the treatment of emotional disorders. The Egyptians and Mesopotamians—like many people even in modern times—believed that diseases, including mental problems, were manifestations of demonic influences. Many early Jews believed that God caused illness as a form of punishment and that mental illness was brought on by particularly evil actions. The author of 6:5 in the Book of Deuteronomy, for example, warned that "The Lord will smite thee with madness." Some religious writers in the Judaic tradition had relatively sophisticated ideas about emotional problems, however. They stressed that mentally disturbed people should be encouraged to talk at length about their problems, enabling them to come to grips with what caused the problems and to help relieve the symptoms.

The most advanced thinking on the mind and mental illness in ancient times came from the Greeks. *Philosophers, scholars,* and *physicians* of this great culture were among the first to seek natural, rather than demonic, causes for mental disorders. The Greek physician Hippocrates (460-377 B.C.) noted that explanations of mental illness based on such concepts as possession of the mind or body by a god, spirit, or demon were a product of ignorance, lacking any real understanding of the natural progression of events. His classification of mental illness—probably the first ever offered—included descriptions of different types of temperaments in individuals.

Greek philosophers focused on the *psyche* (mind, soul, or self) and how it relates to the body. Aristotle's writings on *De Anima* (*The Soul*) synthesized much of the psychological understanding of the time. The Romans, inheriting a rational approach to mental illness from the Greeks, continued to study the problem in those terms. The famous Roman physician, Galen, studied the subject extensively and essentially agreed with Hippocrates on the causes and proper treatment (although treatment was nearly nonexistent at the time) of mental illness.

Despite the rational approach of Greek and Roman scholars, most Greeks and Romans continued to perceive mental diseases as being caused by evil spirits or the wrath of the Furies (the three Greek goddesses of vengeance). The plays of Sophocles made frequent reference to god-sent madness, and many physicians (even Galen) thought that supernatural healing alone could cure the insane. A non-rationalist cult of *priest-physicians*—similar to those of earlier Egypt—also developed in Greek and Roman times; some of these priest-physicians tried to heal the mind as well as the body with treatments combining rest, diet, massage, exercise, and bathing.

Ancient Chinese and Hindu priest-physicians also treated the mentally ill in temples; the Chinese had special institutions for the insane as early as the 12th century B.C. While the "treatments" offered were humane, they were hardly well-developed or organized into actual therapies.

Much the same could be said of Greek treatments, although the Greeks did have somewhat more organized programs for rehabilitation. The Greek temple therapies depended heavily upon mental suggestions or "incubations" that the priest-physicians hoped would eventually cure the sick mind. Sick patients were encouraged to identify with the legendary god Asclepius through dreams or direct contact—the priest being the medium. The priest or an attendant would occasionally practice ventriloquism to help the patient's spirit reach Asclepius, who, it was believed, would either cure the patient or indicate a subsequent treatment. Patients were encouraged to dream as part of the incubation treatment, so that those dreams could then be interpreted.

Non-Asclepian Greco-Roman physicians generally followed the lead of Hippocrates in treating mental illness as a natural disease that, once understood, could be handled. Even so, their treatments left much to be desired. First-century A.D. physician Aulus Cornelius Celsus, who seems to have first used the term *insania* (insanity), used treatments ranging from enemas, massages, and herbal potions to tying up and even torturing severely afflicted patients. Like others for centuries to come, Celsus's stance toward his patients varied from calm sensitivity to frustration and desperation over patients who failed to get well.

The rise of Christianity and the subsequent collapse of the Roman Empire brought the Dark Ages to Europe. The work of those who sought to ease the symptoms of the mentally disturbed virtually ceased. In the early Middle Ages, however, this did not mean special hardship for the insane. Those afflicted were considered unfortunate and deserving of the kindness and gentle caring that good Christians were obliged to confer upon their fellow humans. During this period treatment used for mental illness—and indeed, for most diseases—amounted to little more than meeting basic physical needs.

Later, however, this compassionate attitude disappeared and the old idea that insanity was the direct result of demonic possession and evil influence reappeared. This attitude prevailed among the general population and the healers as well. An odd assortment of people claimed powers as healers. As late as 1602, European healers were described in *The Anatomyes of the True Physition and Counterfeit Montebanks* as "runagate Jews . . . slowbellied monks, who have made escape from their cloisters . . . unlettered chemists . . . lightheaded and trivial druggers and apothecaries . . . stage-players, jugglers, peddlers, prittle-prattling barbers . . . curious bath keepers . . . bragging soldiers, lazy clowns, one-eyed or lamed fencers, toothless and tattling old wives . . . ." Among these charlatans were some who claimed to specialize in removing stones from the head to cure mental illness. (That is presumably the origin of the phrase "rocks in the head.") In some parts of the world such "operations" continued to be performed into the 20th century, with the practitioner producing a small stone as evidence of his success. Added to this band of incompetents were the more sincere but largely ineffective *astrologers, alchemists, nuns,* and *monks,* who generally knew far less about healing than had the ancients.

The treatment of mental illness entered its darkest period. Many hospices (which later developed into hospitals as we know them) refused to accept insane patients. By the 13th and 14th centuries, many so-called healers had resorted to torture and murder to exorcise the evil forces thought to be possessing the insane. Such attitudes toward emotional disorders led to the writing

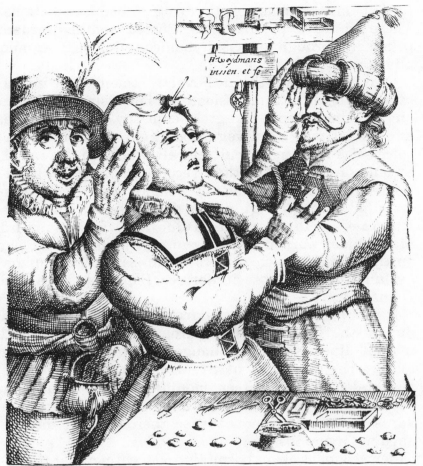

loopt loopt met groot verblyden, Hier salmen twyf van kye snyden..

For thousands of years, charlatans pretend to have cured mental illness by cutting "stones" out of the patient's head. (By H. Weydmans, Dutch, early 17th century, reproduced from Medicine and the Artist, *by permission of the Philadelphia Museum of Art)*

of the *Malleus Maleficarum,* or *The Witch's Hammer,* which Pope Innocent VIII and two monks pieced together in 1484 as a guide to seeking out and destroying witches and those with mental illnesses of unknown cause. Thousands of people—many mentally impaired, often women and children—were tortured and burned at the stake because of this edict, which purported to have as its goal the salvation of Christianity. Monks and other churchmen became the main persons involved in analyzing and "treating" problems of the mind; physicians turned almost exclusively to caring for bodily afflictions. These primitive "psychiatrists" treated mental disorders primarily through exorcism, magico-religious rites, and physical torture.

Only in Islam was the medieval treatment of the insane at all rational or compassionate. Many Islamic healers and asylum keepers had great empathy for the insane, and sometimes even regarded them as divinely inspired—as have many cultures elsewhere in the world. Strongly influenced by the Greco-Roman medical tradition—much of which Islamic healers preserved, while "pagan" records were being destroyed in Christian Europe—scholars like Avicenna, Rhazes, and Maimonides worked seriously in psychotherapy. Acting on their beliefs, such healers set up several exemplary asylums, notably those at Morocco, Baghdad, Cairo, and Damascus.

It was partly through contact with the Islamic world during the Crusades that European attitudes toward mental illness began to change. The military nursing order, the Knights of St. John, also called the Hospitalers, began to accept mentally ill patients at their Jerusalem hospital. (When the Knights retreated from Jerusalem, the Moslems turned their hospital into an asylum for the insane.)

Revised ideas about hospitals and treatment for the insane spread only slowly. A community for the treatment of mental patients developed around a Christian shrine in Gheel, Belgium, where patients congregated and were taken in by local families. Unfortunately, this early pattern of foster-family care was not adopted elsewhere and had little influence on mental treatment—although Gheel itself has continued to be dedicated to psychiatric care, having been granted status as a separate colony within Belgium in the 1850s.

Elsewhere in Europe, change came only gradually. Not until the 14th century were insane asylums established, the earliest and best known being Bethelehem Hospital in London (better known as "Bedlam"). At such hospitals, non-violent patients were often sent out to beg for their keep. When they were released, either for the day or indefinitely, they were given arm badges to wear, so that they could easily be identified and returned to the hospital if they got into trouble. Indeed, by this time, the public's attitude toward mental patients had so changed that many vagrants counterfeited these arm badges in order to get equally good treatment. Despite these improvements, however, views of mental illness still mixed the irrational with the compassionate.

The basis for modern psychology and psychiatry began to be laid during the Scientific Revolution of the 16th and 17th centuries, when the magic of astrology and alchemy and the religious dogma of the Church were first seriously questioned on rational grounds. In 1565 Johann Weyer, called the founder of modern psychiatry, wrote a book with the bold idea that mental illness was a natural disorder and not a demonic possession or divine punishment. In the 17th century, Galileo, Descartes, Hobbes, and many others pointed scientists toward measurement and quantification rather than witch hunts. As people began to rely increasingly on reason to understand the phenomena of sickness and health, the mind itself—or as the Greeks had called it, the *psyche*—became the focus of special studies and discourses. The world *psychology* (literally, study of the mind or psyche) first appeared in a dictionary of physiological terminology in 1693.

In the 18th century, the science began to mature. Christian Von Wolff's *Psychologia Empirica* (1738), employing physiological and behavioral studies, contributed to the growing reliance on scientific approaches to understanding the mind. Early philosophers, scientists, and scholars dabbling in psychological studies were freely criticized by their peers and by churchmen of all faiths. It was bad enough, the critics argued, that biochemists and physiologists had reduced man's body to a cross section to be studied under the microscope, but now even his mind was subject to irreverent abuse.

Fashionable visitors, like the two ladies right of center, often came to asylums to be amused by the insane. (Bedlam Hospital, London, by William Hogarth, National Library of Medicine, Bethesda, Maryland)

Nonetheless, the science of psychology continued to grow in the 18th and 19th centuries. Although he was not a physician, Immanuel Kant devised a classification of mental illnesses in the late 18th century; this classification profoundly influenced the growth and direction of psychology; Kant examined such states of mind as "senselessness," "madness," "absurdity," and "frenzy." Despite taking a basically scientific approach to the subject, Kant was not immune from the superstitious and magical attitudes of his time; he was convinced that the state of "frenzy" could be induced "merely from the staring gaze of a madman."

Johannes Müller carefully scrutinized the nervous system, describing its functioning and noting its relationship to the processes of thinking and perceiving. It was one of Müller's early students—Wilhelm Wundt—who is thought to have been the first actual "psychologist." In his laboratory, established in Leipzig in 1879, Wundt carried out a series of controlled studies and measurements designed to assess personality traits and study the process of perception. It was a bold attempt to apply new discoveries in mathematics and quantification methods to an area historically shrouded in mystery.

Psychologists such as Edward B. Titchener tried to explain behavior by analyzing the structure of the mind, dividing consciousness into images, thoughts, and

By the 19th century, psychiatrists were allowing their patients to go unchained, as here at St. Luke's Hospital in London. (By Thomas Rowlandson and August Pugin, reproduced from Medicine and the Artist, *by permission of the Philadelphia Museum of Art)*

feelings. The school of structuralism was the primary force in psychology until it was eclipsed by that of functionalism. Functionalism—first set forth by William James at Harvard University in 1875—held that behavior was the result of complicated interrelated processes that could not be fully understood simply by analyzing supposed structures of the mind. In the 20th century, the Gestalt school of thought rose to prominence. It held that behavior is organized into unified patterns.

While some psychologists saw behavior strictly in terms of what a person feels or thinks about a situation, others began to consider how one *responds* to a situation. The resulting school of behaviorism accounted for broader and more integrated patterns of behavior than the structuralists had posed. But behaviorists tended to view human behavior purely in terms of stimulus and response, giving little attention to such questions as a person's particular mode of perception or prejudices. While the Gestaltists were interested in exploring the many variables that went into forming personality and motivating behavior, the behaviorists were primarily concerned with the pragmatic task of controlling behavior, based on stimulus-response and learning theories.

Ivan Pavlov's famous series of conditioning experiments, begun in 1904, fueled the behaviorist contention that most learning, and therefore most behavior, is the result of a response to a stimulus. John B. Watson, the father of behaviorism, insisted that psychologists had to be more concerned with the pragmatic results of response rather than with abstract models of structures of the mind. Later behaviorists, such as B. F. Skinner, took behavioral principles to the extreme, indicating that psychologists, by appropriately manipulating a set of stimuli, may thereby control the responses and hence behavior of their subjects. With this power seemingly available to psychologists, many observers worried about the moral implications of such conditioning.

The Gestalt and later experimental psychologists became much more concerned with the complexity of the personality rather than its simple stimulus-response behavior. This research of the "whole person" has had profound effects, particularly on clinical and therapeutic treatments of personality and of mental disorders.

While some psychologists focused on the scientific study of behavior, many others were involved in the therapeutic treatment of patients. Before the 20th century, no sharp distinctions existed between psychology and psychiatry; mental healers were generally scientists—often physicians—who leaned toward either research or treatment. Philippe Pinel, working in the late 18th century, was the first psychiatrist to attempt to study and treat mental disorders in an organized fashion. He unchained the inmates at the French asylums at Bicêtre and Salpêtrière and moved them from dungeons into sunny rooms. He was determined to treat mental patients with kindness and understanding rather than stern reprimands, torture, and exorcism. In England, the Quaker William Tuke established the pleasant, rural York Retreat as an alternative to the dark dungeons for the insane of London. Benjamin Rush, meanwhile, was trying to organize the training of psychiatrists in America. He insisted that doctors treat the mentally ill humanely, although his limited understanding led him to recommend the use of bloodletting and purgatives as part of that "enlightened" therapy.

Toward the close of the 19th century, Emil Kraepelin divided psychosis into manic-depressive and schizophrenic categories, while Jean Martin Charcot researched the structural diseases of the nervous system. Charcot and Pierre Janet both performed clinical experiments to determine the nature of hysteria and the workings of hypnotism. Hypnotism had been developed nearly a century earlier by a physician named Mesmer, who had become enthralled with the use of "animal magnetism"—later called "mesmerism" and then hypnotism—in the treatment of certain psychosomatic disorders.

Important and seminal work, with profound effects on

the development of both psychiatry and psychology, was under taken by Sigmund Freud in the early 20th century. He was the first to recognize formally the significant role that unconscious attitudes and motivations play in human behavior. Freud's analysis of the unconscious led to the development of *psychoanalysis*—in which a patient explores problems and their causes in guided conversation with skilled psychotherapists—as a treatment for various neurotic and psychotic disorders. With Freud the work of psychologists and psychiatrists began to be taken more seriously by both scholars and healers. Dorothea Dix and others paved the way for the mental hygiene movement that became so prominent in the early 20th century.

At the same time, the professions of psychologist and psychiatrist began to diverge. In modern times a psychologist is a person trained in understanding mental processes but not trained in medicine; a psychiatrist is a medical doctor who is qualified to treat mental and emotional as well as physical illness. The distinction between the two professions is essentially highlighted by the psychiatrist's ability (and often inclination) to use drugs in treating his patients. Psychiatry itself was accepted as a branch of modern medicine just before and especially after World War II, when thousands of young men were released from military duty with psychological as well as physical wounds and illnesses.

Many therapies for the treatment of the mentally and emotionally ill have been developed in the last century. Psychiatrists and psychologists alike have become involved in behavioral or behavior-modification therapies designed primarily to get the patient to act in a desired way, regardless of the causes of his improper conduct. Drug therapy and shock therapy have become especially important in this sort of approach. Many observers are cautious or even openly critical of the use of such treatments as insulin coma and electroconvulsive therapy, which is essentially brain shocks administered to alter and control a patient's behavior. Equally con-

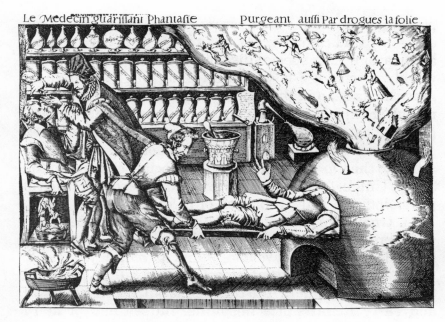

Le Medecin guariffant Phantafie   Purgeant auffi Par drogues la folie.

Like the 17th-century French doctors satirized here, psychiatrists today use drugs and shocks in attempts to "cure fantasy." (Reproduced from Medicine and the Artist, *by permission of the Philadelphia Museum of Art)*

troversial in the past few years has been the use—some say abuse—of drugs used to sedate and stupefy the private patient or institutional inmate (the latter being almost totally at the mercy of his healer). More benign and less invasive treatments include Gestalt therapy, group and individual psychotherapy, existential therapy, and experiential therapy. Psychiatrists and psychologists are apt to use any one or several of these, and psychiatrists often use them along with drug treatments.

Most clinical treatments are based on the experimental efforts of the *research psychologist,* who studies the activities of living things, their interactions in groups, sense perceptions, learning behaviors, and so forth. Clearly, the work of both psychologists and psychiatrists is closely, sometimes inseparably, related, even though they exist as two separate professions. In general, the psychiatrist is a medical doctor who practices in a clinical setting, while a psychologist attains a doctorate or a therapy certificate in his special field and then enters a private therapy practice, or conducts research or teaches in an academic setting. Psychologists spend a greater portion of their time conducting statistical studies, then assessing and comparing data that may have a practical application. As a special discipline, in many parts of the world, psychology is only still emerging. Its greatest growth has been in the United States, where much of the recent emphasis has been on psychotherapy. Elsewhere, physical causes for emotional problems have often been given more weight, and psychology is often more closely allied to the life sciences than to the social sciences. In the Soviet Union, for instance, it is still considered a branch of physiology; in Italy, a branch of medicine.

As treatment of the mentally ill has become more widespread and institutionalized, various specialties have developed in psychology and psychiatry. Indeed, the oldest specialty, that of *psychiatric nurse,* predated the reentry of healers into the field. Controlling medieval and early Renaissance hospitals, nurses had primary responsibility for patients, including the insane. Psychiatric nurses—many of them men, whose physical strength was often necessary to restrain a violent patient—continued to be a major nursing specialty even after the scientific revolution brought physicians into control of the hospital system.

Clinical psychologists and psychiatrists usually treat people with mental or emotional problems, either in private practices or through various government and community agencies, such as mental-hygiene clinics and Veterans Administration hospitals. *Counseling psychologists* use interviewing and testing techniques to help people with "normal" adjustment difficulties related to such things as careers, education, or social interaction. This category includes marriage counselors, drug and alcohol counselors, employment counselors, and counselors for battered wives and abused children, often overlapping with the modern social worker's domain. *Industrial psychologists* do "applied" as opposed to "pure" research to solve practical problems related to business and production. Those that handle personnel situations may be involved in the selection, placement, promotion, supervision, and management of employees; those hand-ling consumer affairs advise companies on advertising, marketing, and public relations.

Modern *educational psychologists* measure education-al achievement, as well as instructional and school administrative quality and efficiency, usually in colleges and universities. *School psychologists* are usually employed by elementary and secondary public school systems. They provide diagnostic and psychotherapeutic services for students while working closely with parents, teachers, and school administrators. *Development psychologists* undertake both pure and applied research related to child development for the benefit of parents, schools, and day-care centers.

Social psychologists apply psychological knowledge and devise statistical studies and measurement techniques to help solve social problems such as marital and family conflicts, racial tensions, crime, juvenile delinquency, and international conflict. *Human* or *psychological engineers* conduct applied research projects, design equipment, and create environments to promote efficiency and safety within special settings—usually military or industrial organizations. *Experimental psychologists* are usually teachers in colleges and universities, who introduce students to the methodologies of pure research and develop specific projects of their own.

Outside the professions of psychiatry and psychology proper, there are many closely related professions that make extensive use of psychiatric techniques and psychological data. Most notable of these is the *social worker,* who undertakes considerable training in psychology and psychotherapy in preparing to deal with special social groups or classes. *Teachers* of the physically and learning disabled, mentally retarded, and gifted also often receive training in psychotherapeutic techniques, to help special groups of learners deal with unusual emotional stress. Specialists have also emerged from the fields of art and music. While these subjects first became standard parts of public school curricula in the 19th century, in the current century *art and music therapists* have come to form part of the support staffs in prisons, hospitals, and psychiatric wards and clinics.

Although significant strides have been taken in the last two centuries in the more successful and humane treatment of the mentally ill, emotionally disturbed, learning disabled, and mentally retarded, a great deal of public prejudice still exists against these populations. Such patients are still too frequently found to be ill-treated or abused in mental institutions, nursing homes, group homes, and elsewhere—sometimes by the very professionals employed to care for them. The great power wielded by psychiatric workers also creates some special problems. In some areas, notably in the Soviet Union, psychiatric incarceration is used as a "treatment" for social or political dissidents, for example. Even where such power is not deliberately abused, however, this virtually unlimited control by the staff in mental institutions—and the enormous, often distorting, role played by psychiatric experts in modern legal defenses—is increasingly coming into question. The manifest uncertainties in the diagnosis and treatment of mental illnesses make such "expert" and often contradictory testimony a source of confusion and public hostility toward the profession. The future of psychiatry and psychology depends on how well its practitioners are able to unite theory and practice into a workable, coherent approach to mental problems.

For related occupations in this volume, *Healers,* see the following:
Nurses
Physicians and Surgeons

For related occupations in other volumes of the series, see the following:
in *Helpers and Aides:*
Social Workers
in *Scholars and Priests:*
Priests

Veterinarians

The Code of Hammurabi, dating back to around 2100 B.C., outlined a scale of fees for *veterinarians*. These early doctors of animals received low pay compared to doctors of people. But then treating animals was less hazardous—only a monetary fine was assessed for losing an animal patient, while a physician risked having his hands cut off for allowing an aristocratic patient to die.

In the ancient world the veterinary profession reached its highest level of development and social standing in India. Exact and extensive records of veterinary procedures and professional practices were carefully preserved for posterity during the Vedic period (1800-1200 B.C.). The profession was greatly respected, for animal life itself was revered, as in most periods of Indian history. Salihotra, a highly accomplished veterinarian,

*This Indian blacksmith, shoeing a bullock with assistants and onlookers, was working much as his counterparts did 2,000 years earlier. (*Illustrated London News, *19th century)*

was regarded almost as a saint. Diagnoses and treatments of illnesses were far ahead of the rest of the world in variety, scope, and accuracy. The profession also had an advanced system of specialization and ethics. The earliest known animal hospitals were built and staffed with veterinarians during the reign of the Buddhist King Asoka in the third century B.C.

The Chinese, farther east, also honored veterinarians. One Chinese veterinarian, Ma Shih-huang, was renowned for his skill in treating horses. According to myth he also healed dragons, which bore him away to their lair in grateful thanks.

In Egypt, the papyrus of Kahun dating back to about 1900 B.C., speaks highly of the profession of animal doctors. There appear to have been very few there, however.

Elsewhere in the ancient world, veterinarians had a rather low social status. They were lowly practitioners, largely uneducated and drawn from the commonest lot of herdsmen and poulterers. The most prestigious animal tenders in Classical times were those that the Greeks called *hippiatroi,* or doctors of horses. The Romans called the horse doctor *equarius medicus.* Horses were extremely important for agriculture and travel, but especially for war, so their care was essential and therefore somewhat respectable.

Aristotle's *History of Animals* (333 B.C.) was the first noteworthy Western work about animals, a collection of observations about their habits, anatomies, and associated lore. For instance, one part notes that cattle prefer to drink clear water, while horses prefer muddy water. Book VIII of the work includes observations about veterinary medicine; for example, it describes some of the simple symptoms of tetanus. Others also wrote on animal care, particularly relating to the breeding and training of horses.

The Romans added little to this basic body of knowledge. Varro reported in 36 B.C. that very few people knew how to care for animals. For the most part, shepherds, farmers, and priests offered sick animals only domestic cures, prayers, and magic rituals or incantations. Varro noted that skilled help was provided only in very special cases and then usually by a general physician. The veterinary profession did not grow much until the latter days of the empire when horse doctors were needed to tend military horses. The Roman *veterinarius* was the doctor who cared for beasts of burden in addition to war horses. Regiments of the later empire often had a *veterinarium* or hospital for sick and wounded horses.

During the Middle Ages, the veterinary profession flourished in the Moslem world. Moslem (Islamic) scholars greatly emphasized horse warfare. Their scholars tirelessly copied and preserved Classical literature, much of which was lost in Europe during the Dark Ages. Although the importance of horsemanship gave the profession an elevated status, the Moslems broke little new ground in terms of medical or surgical knowledge in the field. Ibn-al-Awam was the most important Islamic veterinarian scholar. His *Book of Agriculture,* written in the 12th century, was one of the landmark works in the field before the invention of the printing press.

Although written centuries earlier, the most important works dealing with veterinary practices went largely unappreciated until after the European Renaissance. *Artis Veterinariae* (*The Veterinary Art*), written by the Roman scholar Vegetius in the fifth century A.D., was not widely recognized until it became the first printed book on the subject in 1528. Vegetius openly applauded the efforts of veterinarians, while bemoaning the ill repute that they suffered as a class and as a profession. Vegetius himself was a significant contributor to knowledge in the field, emphasizing the importance of hygiene and prevention as well as the quarantining of sick animals. The first writer of the Christian era to devote an entire book to veterinary medicine, Vegetius has been called the "veterinary Hippocrates."

Five hundred years after Vegetius, during the 10th-century reign of Constantine Porphyrogenitus of Byzantium, a great summary of the veterinary medical art was compiled into a work called the *Hippiatrika*. The profession gained considerable prestige during this period in the Near East and was extremely active and well organized. One of the authorities cited frequently in the *Hippiatrika* was Apsyrtus, a Byzantine veterinarian of the fourth century A.D. who has sometimes been given the title "father of veterinary medicine." His knowledge apparently surpassed that of any others in the profession before modern times. The profession being largely hereditary at the time, his family carried on his knowledge until it was entered into the *Hippiatrika* many generations after his death.

The later Middle Ages marked a low point for the veterinary profession. Methods of diagnosis and techniques of surgery and cure were carefully controlled by the Roman Catholic Church, which had a rather cold

Like most healers of his time, this 16th-century veterinarian carried his tools and medicines slung from his belt. (Authors' archives)

attitude toward animal life. Accordingly, appeals to the saints, magical rituals, and mysterious incantations had become the chief "cures" of the day.

Beginning in the 11th century, during the Age of Chivalry, tournaments and cavalry installations in various armies began to place considerable emphasis on horsemanship. The Crusades began at about the same time and a further respect for the horse was soon gained from exposure to the Moslems. The horseshoe, originally devised by the Romans, was refined to make horses more dependable than ever before for work, transportation, and war. In fact, the horseshoer, or *farrier,* was the most common "horse doctor" for many centuries.

In the same period, "hawking" was a popular sport among feudal lords and aristocrats. *Hawk doctors* made regular rounds for some years, many being taken in and patronized by their lords. The increasing economic significance of the wool industry in England, along with frequent and devastating cattle plagues and sheep-pox and anthrax outbreaks, gave the professional cattle doctor, or *"cow leech,"* a chance to peddle his skills and cures. Other practitioners specialized in certain kinds of operations, like hog gelding; some of these were all-purpose knife-wielders who were called in by *midwives* to cut apart dead unborn babies, so they could be extracted in pieces from the mother's womb.

In some areas, though, especially in the Byzantine Empire, veterinary medicine became quite advanced, at least in relation to human medicine. Unlike physicians, veterinarians were free to do exploratory dissections or post-mortem examinations. Much pioneer anatomical work was done by veterinarians, especially in Italy. In fact, much of the knowledge that veterinarians accumulated was borrowed by physicians and found its way into the practice and literature related to humans. Veterinary medicine remained more advanced than human medicine for many centuries. However, it was not until the invention of the printing press and the subsequent publication of the *Artis Veterinariae* (printed at Basel) and the *Hippiatrika* (printed at Paris) between 1528 and 1530 that the profession was truly delivered from its Dark Ages.

The *Artis Veterinariae* was particularly significant, for it insisted on natural rather than demonic causes of animal diseases. Writing in the fifth century, Vegetius had ridiculed those people who insisted that God's wrath caused illnesses and he spoke in glowing terms of how the veterinarian could intervene to help alleviate such afflictions. In fact, he was clearly distressed at the way his profession had been so recklessly criticized by the public and by physicians, with their ill-founded sense of superiority. In the thousand years between the writing and the publication of *Artis Veterinariae,* matters had only become worse. Medieval Christianity often portrayed animal life in terms of evil, since animals apparently obeyed no divine or moral law, but only that of nature. The publication of Vegetius, then, was a great benefit to the profession and its slowly recovering social status.

Farriers often used structures like this one to hold a horse in place for shoeing or dosing. (By Jost Amman, from Künstbuchlin, 1599)

During the 16th century, the number of veterinarians increased, a great many of them being patronized by nobility and even royalty. Ferdinand and Isabella of Aragon and Castile, in Spain, even developed professional schools for the training of veterinarians and examination systems for the official licensing of practitioners. In 1531 one writer observed that the occupation had become "more profitable" than many others, even though it was still held in general disrepute by most "fine physicians." One reason that the profession continued to be scorned was that most animal "doctors," right up to the 19th century, were untrained farriers and cow leeches.

The farriers, easily the more prestigious and profitable of the two groups, were usually uneducated in any formal sense. Their learning came only through their apprenticeship to the blacksmith's trade. This was typically a family affair. Herbal lotions and magic incantations believed to be particularly effective against specific diseases were held in the strictest confidence and used with the utmost mystery by all family members. These lotions and incantations were passed on from generation to generation, generally through the male line, but sometimes through the females of the family. Farriers were often cited for cheating their clients and overcharging them for useless treatments. Nonetheless, many were patronized by wealthy families and some did quite well financially, especially those attached to cavalries. Cow leeches were even more scorned than the farriers, who ridiculed cow leeches for treating farm beasts, such as swine, rather than the glorious horse. Veterinarians were closely associated with these two bungling and inept occupations. Indeed, there was frequently little real difference in practice between the educated, trained veterinarian and the farrier or cow leech.

Perhaps the most important figure in the maturity of the profession was Carlo Ruini. With his *Anatomy of the Horse, Diseases and Treatment* (1598), this Italian aristocrat founded modern veterinary *science* (rather than *art,* as the care of sick animals had previously been termed). Ruini made extensive use of careful dissections in pioneering the field of equine anatomy. His great understanding of anatomy, especially his detailed descriptions of the pulmonary circulation and reproductive systems of the horse, allowed him to take a truly scientific approach to the cure of disease and injury. Unfortunately, few veterinarians of the time took advantage of Ruini's discoveries or followed up his research. Still, his work at least convinced the leading practitioners that the scientific approach was the proper one, even if few practical gains immediately resulted.

The 17th century was a time of half-baked, pseudoscientific notions handed down from one writer to another, resulting in total confusion among practitioners and theorists alike. Perhaps the greatest offender to scientific integrity was Gervase Markham, whose famous works on veterinary practices (most notably *The English*

Husbandman) set the tone for the next hundred years. Markham made outlandish claims for supposedly instant cures, once even suggesting he could cure all horse and cattle maladies with only 12 medicines! His works began with long, flowery dedications to his literary patrons, chiefly the Earl of Southampton, and he promised to discuss miraculous cures and new, revolutionary scientific breakthroughs. Yet, no such information was forthcoming. Instead, one found a hodgepodge of misinformation or a rerun of old ideas passed off as new ones. In many cases, supposed breakthroughs in veterinary medicine were glossed over with just a few quick words.

Other writers in the field tended to follow Markham's example, not very surprising since his were the most popular veterinary works of the age. Like Markham, later so-called authorities also promised great things, but delivered little or nothing. They, too, filled their works with old ideas and an abundance of plagiarisms meant to seem revolutionary. The peculiar types of cures recommended by these early veterinary "scientists" reflected the scarcity of accurate scientific information circulating in the professional ranks. For example, one anonymous writer in the late 17th century sought to cure a horse disease known as "mourning of the chine" by bleeding the horse, pouring certain medicines down its nostrils, and then closing the nostrils so that the horse "may be forced to sneeze and strain to cast it out."

Given this climate, the veterinary profession progressed slowly. The few forward-looking and truly scientific men of the profession, like Sir William Hope in Britain, publicly deplored the lack of skilled practitioners. Indeed, semi-skilled and unskilled practitioners predominated. Cow leeches, horsetrainers, blacksmiths, and farriers continued to act in a sort of semi-professional capacity. Even so, farriers were as good as and sometimes better than the schooled veterinarians of the time. Many farriers were skilled (by the standards of that time) in surgical procedures and suturing; one of

While veterinary science was developing, practitioners such as this 19th-century Siberian blacksmith, continued to care for most draft animals. (The Century Illustrated Monthly Magazine)

them—Thomas Bishop, the younger, of Wallingford, England—performed the first recorded successful intestinal surgery on a horse during the 1690s.

Leaders in the scientific movement—often gentlemen of leisure—seldom received a sympathetic hearing from farriers, who were usually working men with little time or inclination toward theoretical research. Farriers also feared competition; as leading veterinary scientist J. L. de Solleysel was fond of reminding French farriers, there were as many veterinarians in Germany as there were physicians in all of France. When Solleysel recommended radical changes and standard guidelines in treatment procedures, Parisian farriers rebelled. Anxious to guard the long-held family secrets that made their services exclusive, they insisted that Solleysel's reforms were unnecessary. Despite the efforts of Solleysel and others, the profession remained largely in the hands of the farriers for another century and a half.

During the 18th century, becoming increasingly closed and secretive, the ignorant but still arrogant farriers tried to compete with the rising numbers of educated veterinarians. Apprenticeships became more restrictive and demanding, and masters divulged family trade secrets only after several years' training. Physicians continued to criticize veterinarians, claiming that they—like the farriers and cattle doctors—were usually "men without education, dependent upon tradition and perhaps a book of 'cures'...." They were largely correct, of course, but were hardly the people to pass such judgments, for the medical profession itself was still considerably backward.

Ultimately, the greatest stimulus to the veterinary profession, was the devastating series of cattle plagues that rocked Europe between 1710 and 1760, when some 200 million cattle died from "rinderpest" or the "cattle plague." Farriers and cow leeches were of no help during these serious epidemics, and physicians and veterinarians were called on by various governments to deal with the problem. For a long time, little progress was made. Physicians were reluctant and embarrassed by the prospect of working on animals, and veterinarians were simply not sufficiently trained for the task. Most research was done on horses rather than cattle since they were more "acceptable" objects of study. Churchmen, meanwhile, preached against medical intervention, which they saw as an attempt to cover up God's wrath against the sins of materialism, pragmatism, and naturalism. Presumed authorities such as the horse owner and physician Henry Bracken continued to sell books offering cheap cures that supposedly anyone could bring about without costly professional help. Meanwhile, the cattle plague raged on.

A few physicians finally stepped forward, encouraging other physicians to lend a hand. But the single greatest assistance came from James Clark of Edinburgh, one time "Farrier to the King of Scotland," later given the title of "Veterinary Professor." Clark criticized heavy drug interventions and the popular technique of excessive bloodletting. He offered instead a more painstaking and scientific approach to the problem—one that he personally used in extensive post-mortem analyses. Rather than consult a recipe book of cures, he argued, the properly educated and trained veterinarian "must first investigate the cause, the nature, and various symptoms attending different diseases that have a resemblance to one another . . . and when he has carefully compared them together he will be able to make a proper distinction and in a great measure to determine the true seat of the disease."

Often called the "Father of Veterinary Hygiene," Clark recommended that the term "veterinarian" be used more routinely to denote the new trend toward scientific investigation over the old "recipe book cures" approach. The new veterinarian, he hoped, would pay greater attention to the prevention of disease through an understanding of proper hygiene and nursing care. He vowed to help alleviate the causes of plagues by properly ventilating stables and barns; by giving animals sufficient fresh air, pure water, and wholesome food; by isolating sick animals; and by reducing the often cruel workload of horses and beasts of burden. Clark's ideas were enlightening to the veterinary profession—and might also have been useful to most physicians of the time.

The most lasting and significant of Clark's suggestions was that the new veterinarian had to be better prepared for practicing his profession. This meant, to Clark and others, that professional training had to be created if there was to be any advancement of the profession. Claude Bourgelat opened the first modern scientific veterinary schools in northern Europe. Both were in France—at Lyons (1761) and at Alfort, near Paris (1765). John Hunter founded the Veterinary School of London in 1791. By 1800 there were 20 such schools in 12 European countries. As the 19th century began, veterinarians trained in these schools were being at least as well prepared for their professions as physicians were for theirs. The first truly clinical studies were under way during the initial half of the century, adding significantly to the general body of knowledge concerning animal care and the treatment of diseases and wounds.

America, isolated geographically, did not suffer from the European cattle plagues. The blacksmith, or farrier, remained the chief veterinarian there until the second half of the 19th century, and the development of the veterinary profession generally lagged well behind its growth in Europe. Only a handful of distinguished European veterinarians were employed in the United States by the time the first North American veterinary school was established, in Guelph, Ontario, in 1862. The Canadian school remained the main source of veterinarians in the United States until the founding of the American Veterinary College (1875) in New York by Francis Alexander Liautard.

Since the horse was still the chief means of transportation, hauling, and farm work, and was indispensable in war, most veterinarians of the 19th and early 20th centuries were horse doctors. But the invention and mass production of automobiles, tractors, trucks, and airplanes changed the focus of veterinarian training and practice. Wherever transportation was motorized, farriers and other specialists like hog-gelders, disappeared and were replaced by modern, trained veterinarians. Today veterinarians practicing in rural areas of industrialized countries usually have general practices, being prepared to care for most farm animals. Other veterinarians have tended to specialize. Nearly a third of the practitioners in the United States, for example, now specialize in the treatment of small domestic pets like dogs and cats; most of them operate private practices in urban and suburban areas. A few veterinarians even specialize in the treatment of certain exotic animals, such as elephants, lions, or snakes.

Although the great majority of veterinarians are now employed in private practices, other opportunities are available to them. Those employed in public health agencies conduct research, inspect the quality of meats, and supervise the treatment and prevent the abuse of racing and domestic animals as well as wildlife. Some veterinarians work with special animal populations like

Before automobiles took over the hauling duties performed by horses, special ambulances were devised to carry exhausted, ill, or injured horses to veterinary help. (By W. P. Bodfish, Harper's Weekly, January 14, 1888)

those in zoos, in wildlife reserves, or on farm factories. Animals held for slaughter, dairying, and the like require special attention; those raised in unhealthy factorylike conditions are extremely susceptible to diseases and injury. Veterinarians are employed to try to control contagious diseases in these settings; they tend to the welfare of the herd or flock as a whole with a great array of vaccinations and antibiotics (which ultimately find their way into meat and dairy products sold to consumers). Some veterinarians work for private industries such as fox and minx furriers in the management of large groups of such animals. Many more are employed by large commercial pharmaceutical companies and research laboratories in the testing of drugs and vaccines on animals.

The veterinary profession today represents a highly respectable and affluent career choice, nearly on a par with that of the physician. Only in the underdeveloped countries (where animal diseases and epidemics generally go unchecked) does the profession languish, as it did for so many centuries in the West. Veterinarians are organized in countless local, state, regional, and national associations throughout the world. The American Veterinary Medical Association (AVMA), originally founded in 1863 by practitioners from both Canada and the United States, is now the largest of its kind in the world. The International Veterinary Congress, which convenes every four years, is represented by some 60 countries.

Veterinarians have gained considerable respect and opportunity in the last century, as animals have been given increasing attention and protection. Wildlife protection agencies, pet adoption centers, and humane societies have all come to the aid of animals around the world. Even farm animals raised for slaughter and dairying have recently become the recipients of protective lobbying. The Farm Animal Reform Movement (F.A.R.M.) in Washington, D.C., expresses the purpose of such groups in this way: "to promote reverence for life and to alleviate and eliminate abuses of farm animals and other adverse impacts of animal agriculture on human health, world hunger, and natural resources." The rising respect for all animal life has contributed significantly to the increasing stature of veterinarians.

For related occupations in this volume, *Healers,* see the following:
  Midwives and Obstetricians
  Physicians and Surgeons

For related occupations in other volumes of the series, see the following:
in *Helpers and Aides:*
  Drivers
in *Manufacturers and Miners:*
  Metalsmiths
in *Warriors and Adventurers:*
  Soldiers

Suggestions for Further Reading

General

Atkinson, Donald T. *Magic, Myth and Medicine*. Freeport, New York: Books for Libraries Press, 1972 (first pub. 1956). Interesting articles on various topics in medical history.

Bettmann, Otto L. *A Pictorial History of Medicine*. Springfield, Illinois: Charles C. Thomas Publisher, 1956. Many short, breezy, illustrated essays on aspects of medicine.

Cartwright, Frederick F. *A Social History of Medicine*. New York: Longman, Inc., 1977. A useful work, mostly on English medical history.

Castiglioni, Arturo. *A History of Medicine.* Translated and edited by E. B. Krumbhaar. New York: Alfred A. Knopf, 1941. A comprehensive general work.

Ghalioungui, Paul. *Magic and Medical Science in Ancient Egypt.* London: Hodder and Stoughton, 1963. A detailed review.

Glassscheib, H. S. *The March of Medicine: The Emergence and Triumph of Modern Medicine.* Translated by Mervin Savill. New York: G. P. Putnam's Sons, 1964. A popularly written general work.

Guthrie, Douglas. *A History of Medicine.* Rev. ed. Philadelphia: J. B. Lippincott Co., 1958. An excellent general work that focuses in the modern section on discoverers.

Kutumbiah, P. *Ancient Indian Medicine.* Madras, India: Orient Longmans Ltd., 1962. A detailed review.

Lyons, Albert S. and R. Joseph Petrucelli. *Medicine: An Illustrated History.* New York: Harry N. Abrams, Inc., 1978. A sound, beautifully illustrated work.

Reiser, Stanley Joel. *Medicine and the Reign of Technology.* New York: Cambridge University Press, 1978. Very useful on overall changes in the modern period.

Sigerist, Henry E. *History of Medicine. Primitive and Archaic Medicine,* vol. 1, *Early Greek, Hindu, and Persian Medicine,* vol. 2. New York: Oxford University Press, 1951; 1961. A prime work, part of a projected eight-volume series, unfinished at the author's death.

Thorwald, Jürgen. *Science and Secrets of Early Medicine: Egypt, Mesopotamia, India, China, Mexico, Peru.* New York: Harcourt, Brace & World, Inc., 1963. Contains separate detailed chapters on each region.

Walker, Kenneth. *The Story of Medicine*. New York: Oxford University Press, 1955. A good general overview.

Wong, K. Chimin and Wu Lien Te. *History of Chinese Medicine*. Shanghai: National Quarantine Service, 1936. New York: AMS Press, 1973 (reprint, 2nd ed.). A comprehensive standard work.

Zimmer, H. R. *Hindu Medicine*. Baltimore, Md.: Johns Hopkins University Press, 1948. Very useful essays, unfinished at the author's death.

Barbers

Andrews, William. *At the Sign of the Barber's Pole: Studies in Hirsute History*. Detroit: Singing Tree Press, 1969 (first pub. 1904). An indiscriminate collection of anecdotes.

Cooper, Wendy. *Hair*. New York: Stein and Day, 1971. A popular historical account.

Dentists

Bremner, M. D. K. *The Story of Dentistry*. 3rd ed. New York: Dental Items of Interest Publishing Co., 1954. A useful general history of Western dentistry.

Guerini, Vincenzo. *A History of Dentistry*. Philadelphia: Lea & Febiger, 1909. A classic work that goes only to the 19th century.

Midwives and Obstetricians

Donegan, Jane B. *Women and Men Midwives: Medicine, Morality and Misogyny in Early America.* Westport, Conn.: Greenwood Press, 1978.

Flack, Isaac Harvey. *Eternal Eve: The History of Gynaecology and Obstetrics.* Garden City, New York: Doubleday, 1951. A comprehensive work with international coverage.

Forbes, Thomas R. *The Midwife and the Witch.* New Haven: Yale University Press, 1966. Essays on various topics.

Haggard, Howard W. *Devils, Drugs, and Doctors: The Story of the Science of Healing from Medicine-Man to Doctor.* New York: Harper & Row, 1929. Part One is a history of childbirth practices.

Litoff, Judy Barrett. *American Midwives: 1860 to the Present.* Westport, Conn.: Greenwood Press, 1978.

Nurses

Bullough, Vern and Bonnie Bullough. *The Care of the Sick: The Emergence of Modern Nursing.* New York: Prodist, 1978. A sound history; international overview but modern period has U.S. focus.

Dock, Lavinia L. and Isabel M. Stewart. *A Short History of Nursing, From the Earliest Times to the Present Day.* 4th ed. New York: G. P. Putnam's Sons, 1983. An early study, drawing on Nutting and Dock's classic *A History of Nursing* in 4 volumes, 1902-1912.

Dolan, Josephine A. *Nursing in Society: A Historical Perspective*. 14th ed. Philadelphia: W. B. Saunders Co., 1978. A well-illustrated, anecdotal textbook.

Goldstein, Harold M., and Morris A. Horowitz. *Entry-Level Health Occupations: Development and Future*. Baltimore: Johns Hopkins University Press, 1977.

Greenfield, Harry I. and Carol A. Brown. *Allied Health Manpower: Trends and Prospects*. New York: Columbia University Press, 1969.

Pavey, Agnes E. *The Story of the Growth of Nursing*. 5th ed. London: Faber and Faber Ltd., 1959. A popular account.

Pharmacists

Kremers, Edward, and George Urdang. *History of Pharmacy*. 4th ed. Revised by Glenn Sonnedecker. Philadelphia: J. B. Lippincott Co., 1976. A prime work on modern Western pharmacy, country by country.

Thompson, C. J. S. *The Mystery and Art of the Apothecary*. London: John Lane, Bodley Head Ltd., 1929. A popular and anecdotal review.

Physicians and Surgeons

Albutt, Thomas C. *The Historical Relations of Medicine and Surgery to the End of the 16th Century*. New York: AMS Press, 1976 (first pub. 1905). A classic series of lectures, from a turn-of-the-century perspective.

Haggard, Howard W. *The Doctor in History*. New Haven: Yale University Press, 1924. A popular review of Western doctors.

Hughes, Muriel Joy. *Women Healers in Medieval Life and Literature*. Freeport, New York: Books for Libraries Press, 1968 (first pub. 1943). A fascinating essay on a neglected topic.

Pollak, K. and E. Ashworth Underwood. *The Healers*. London: Thomas Nelson & Sons, Ltd., 1968. An international, historical review.

Shryock, Richard H. *Development of Modern Medicine: An Interpretation of the Sociology and Scientific Factors Involved*. New York: Alfred A. Knopf, 1947. A useful review of general practice from 1600 to the mid-20th century.

Unschuld, Paul. *Medical Ethics in Imperial China: A Study in Historical Anthropology*. Berkeley: University of California Press, 1979. A valuable and detailed work.

Psychologists and Psychiatrists

Alexander, Franz G. and Sheldon T. Selesnick. *The History of Psychiatry: An Evaluation of Psychiatric*

Thought and Practice from Prehistoric Times to the Present. New York: Harper & Row, 1966. A general treatment.

Bromberg, Walter. *The Mind of Man: A History of Psychotherapy and Psychoanalysis.* New York: Harper & Row, 1963. Traces the variety of therapies for mental and emotional disorders that have been used since the earliest times.

Doerner, Klaus. *Madmen and the Bourgeoisie: A Social History of Insanity and Psychiatry.* Totowa, N.J.: Biblio Distribution Centre, 1982. Good insight given into the influence that psychiatrists have had on social norms.

Foucault, Michel. *Madness and Civilization: A History of Insanity in the Age of Reason.* New York: Random House, Inc., 1973. Addresses the nature of psychiatry and psychology at the dawn of the modern age.

Herrnstein, Richard J. and Edwin G. Boring, ed. *Sourcebook in the History of Psychology.* Cambridge, Mass.: Harvard University Press, 1965. A general treatment of the subject.

Leahey, Thomas H. *A History of Psychology.* New York: Prentice-Hall, 1980. A general treatment of the subject.

Roback, Abraham A. *History of Psychology and Psychiatry.* Westport, Conn.: Greenwood Press, 1961. A good review of the evolution of these closely related fields.

Scull, Andrew, ed. *Madhouses, Mad-Doctors, and Madmen: The Social History of Psychiatry in the Victorian Era.* Philadelphia: University of Pennsylvania Press, 1981. A look at the status of the profession just before the 20th century and the revolutionary advances of the social sciences.

Simon, Bennett. *Mind and Madness in Ancient Greece: The Classical Roots of Modern Psychiatry*. Ithaca, N.Y.: Cornell University Press, 1978. Considers the role of the psychiatrist in ancient Greek society.

Veterinarians

Careers: Working with Animals. Washington, D.C.: Acropolis Books, 1979. Prepared by the Humane Society of the United States. Discusses the present state and projected future of the veterinary and related professions.

Smith, Sir Frederick. *The Early History of Veterinary Literature*. 4 volumes. London: Bailliere, Tindall and Cox, 1919. Critical and thorough review of the development of the profession, from the earliest times through the first two-thirds of the 19th century.

Smithcors, James Frederick. *The American Veterinary Profession; Its Background and Development*. Ames, Iowa: Iowa State University Press, 1963. The prime work on the growth of the profession in America.

———. *Evolution of the Veterinary Art*. Kansas City, Mo.: Veterinary Medical Publishing Co., 1957. Has been called "The only complete book on veterinary medical history." Covers the evolution of the "art" up to 1850.

INDEX